History of the Zulu War, 1879

(Facsimile of his Signature on the last Draft drawn by him through the Standard Bank on Messrs. Rothschild & Co.)

NAPOLEON LOUIS BONAPARTE

History of the Zulu War, 1879

A Chronicle of the war by a
commentator on the scene

Alexander Wilmot

LEONAUR

History of the Zulu War, 1879
A Chronicle of the war by a
commentator on the scene
by Alexander Wilmot

First published under the title
History of the Zulu War

Leonaur is an imprint
of Oakpast Ltd

ISBN: 978-0-85706-078-5 (hardcover)
ISBN: 978-0-85706-077-8 (softcover)

http://www.leonaur.com

Publisher's Notes

In the interests of authenticity, the spellings, grammar and place names used have been retained from the original editions.

The opinions of the authors represent a view of events in which he was a participant related from his own perspective, as such the text is relevant as an historical document.

The views expressed in this book are not necessarily those of the publisher.

Contents

PREFATORY NOTE

Blue Books and correspondents' letters necessarily form the principal authorities. The preliminary portion of the book has been really requisite, and it is hoped that it will be found not the least interesting portion of the volume. No doubt, in the first connected narrative of the Zulu war, many omissions and inaccuracies may be discovered, but every effort has been made to collect the truth from the most reliable authorities, and to tell it without fear, favour, or prejudice.

Port Elizabeth,
25th September, 1879.

Chapter 1

Early History of the Zulu Nation and of Natal

Two different races met in Southern Africa about the middle of the seventeenth century. One had migrated from the centre of the continent; the other sent out settlers from one of the most civilized and prosperous countries of Europe. These races were the Kafirs and the Dutch. The former arrived at the banks of the Great Fish River about the same time that Surgeon Van Riebeek landed on the shores of Table Bay for the purpose of establishing "a place of refreshment for the outward and homeward bound fleets of the chartered Dutch East India Company." The progress of the new colony was so gradual and slow that it was not until the nineteenth century that Kafir irruptions were effectually checked, and then the British Government had assumed sovereignty over the Cape of Good Hope.

Different causes, to which it is not necessary to refer, made the descendants of the Dutch settlers so dissatisfied with our rule that a portion of them, in the year 1837, passed into that easterly portion of Southern Africa styled Natal. There they came in contact with the bravest and best-organized portion of the great Kafir race. The Ama-Zulus were originally a small and despised tribe. They were "tobacco sellers," or pedlars, and carried on this occupation at the beginning of the present century in the country between the Black and White Umvolosi Rivers.

In contradistinction to the nature of their employment, and as an emblem of the ambition of the people, the name they gave themselves was one of the proudest they could have chosen, as "the Zulus" in the Kafir tongue signifies "the Celestials." At an early period in this century a great leader arose among them, who became the Genghis Khan of Southern Africa. This chief was fitly named "*Utskaka*"—"*Chaka*," or "Break of Day;" and it was in consequence of his efforts and of his success that a new era commenced for his countrymen.

Chaka was never defeated, and never fled before a foe. Having ascended the throne by means of the murder of his uncle, he proceeded at once to convert a nation of pedlars into a nation of warriors.' Immense care was taken with military training, and the weapon by means of which the Roman soldiers conquered the world was adopted for the use of the army. The short sword, or stabbing *assegai*, was supplied, with the command that each warrior should carry but one, and either bring it back from the battlefield or be put to death as a coward. Marriage was forbidden, although the gratification of brutal lust was allowed. No warrior could have a wife or child to imbue him with any tender sentiment.

The practice of circumcision, although one of the most ancient and important rites, was abandoned, so that everything, no matter how sacred or how important, was sacrificed in order to create invincible legions. The army consisted of three divisions. The first was composed of veterans, styled "*amadoda*," or men; the second of youths, "*ebuto*;" and the third of "*ezibuto*," or carriers. It was in the last division that conquered enemies were frequently enrolled. The king was the commander-in-chief, and under him were the principal *indunas*, or ministers of state. Each regiment was at least 1500 strong, and was led by a captain, who had under him numerous subalterns. Military *kraals* were scattered over the country, generally of an oval shape, and of large dimensions.

Reviews took place at the great place of the king, where songs, dances, and chivalrous games were all made use of to increase the military enthusiasm of the warriors. When war was determined upon, extreme secrecy was observed, spies were sent out, and the usual incantations and sacrifices performed by the priest or witch-doctor. A herald, dressed in the skins of wild beasts, so as to present a terrific appearance, then was sent to the army, and cried with a loud voice, "*Maikupuke!*"—"Go up!" An inspiring oration was delivered by the king, and they went forth to conquer or to die, fifty thousand well-organized, determined savages, giving no quarter, slaying men, women, children, and even domestic animals.

Thus has a warrior described the onset of one of these savage armies:—"The Matabele lions raised the shout of death, and fell upon their victims. It was the shout of victory. Their hissing and hollow

10

groans told their progress among the dead. A few moments laid hundreds on the ground. The clash of shields was the signal of triumph. They entered the town with the roar of the lion; they pillaged and fired the houses, speared the mothers, and cast their infants to the flames. They slaughtered cattle; they danced and sang till the dawn of day; they ascended and killed till their hands were weary of the spear."

Chaka not only led his army in person, but was accustomed himself to seize the first victim, and to kill him with his spear. After subduing the petty tribes around, he bore his victorious arms further, and carried fire and sword along the slopes of the Drakenberg Mountains. One of his greatest conquests was over the Undwandwa people, and this was followed by the destruction of the Umtetwas. An attack was then made upon the brave Amaquabi, who occupied both sides of the Tugela river, which forms the present boundary of Natal. Merciless slaughters followed victory, and the tide of conquest only ceased on the banks of the Umsimvoboo.

In the year 1828, Lieutenant Farewell, Mr. H. Fynn, and a few others, were permitted to visit Chaka, who then resided at a distance of about 150 miles in a north-north-east direction from D'Urban, Port Natal. The Englishmen were received by the mighty Zulu potentate with great ceremony. Nine thousand armed warriors stood around, and the despotic character of the monarch was reflected in the servile submission with which he was treated by his subjects. Chaka munificently granted a large tract of country to Mr. H. Fynn, and subsequently conferred a similar favour upon Lieutenant King. These grants—and all grants of this nature—were, strictly speaking, mere feudal investitures, paramount rights being retained by the monarch. The first European settlement in Natal was thus formed.

An act of treason on the part of one of Chaka's greatest lieutenants alienated him from his native land, and became the means of carrying fire and sword north of the Drakenberg Mountains as far as Bamangwato. Moselekatsi, whom Captain Harris styles the "Lion of the North," was this lieutenant. Wherever he moved destruction and death marked his path, and he soon succeeded in rearing another cruel military despotism over the graves of those whom he had conquered.

The last army of Chaka which went forth to destroy was itself destroyed by one of those strange judgements which bear analogy to that inflicted on the hosts of Sennacherib. A nation dwelling close to the Palula River had to be conquered, but before this place was reached a frightful disease, styled "blood sickness," broke out, and was so fatal in its results that only a few men of the great army were able to return to tell the tale. Scarcely had this event occurred, when the tyrant was himself assassinated. Chaka was seated peacefully in his *kraal*, near the Umvoti River, surrounded by his councillors and principal officers, when a band of desperate men, headed by his brother Dingaan, rushed among them, and each, seizing his victim, plunged a spear into his heart. Thus perished the Napoleon of the Zulu race, by the hand of his own nearest relative, and at a moment when he did not suspect treachery or dream of any insurrection against his well-consolidated power.

Dingaan—"poor fellow!"—was no doubt secretly encouraged by a large portion of the Zulu people. A number of the principal captains and friends of the late monarch fled, and several were put to death. The new capital was removed from the Umvati River to the White Umvolosi River, distant 45 miles in a direct line from the sea, and about 160 miles from D'Urban. The favour that had been extended by Chaka to the few Englishmen who arrived in Natal with Mr. H. Fynn was a sufficient reason for the adoption by his successor of an exactly opposite policy. An army of 3000 men was sent to D'Urban, and the few English settlers escaped with the utmost difficulty. Every vestige of property was destroyed. Quietness was, however, restored in a few years afterwards, and in the year 1833 Dingaan sent down spies to find out what progress had been made by the intruders.

Captain Allen Gardiner arrived in 1835, and proceeded to the great place of the king. This missionary traveller mentions incidentally that, according to treaty, he brought back several men who had fled from the cruel despotism of the Zulu monarch. These captives fully calculated upon being put to death. Captain Gardiner pleaded for them, and was able to assure them that the king had promised to spare their lives. Nowha, one of the unfortunate prisoners, mournfully replied, "They are killing us now;" and they were all cruelly tortured to death by starvation.[1]

In consequence of various causes, among which discontent with British rule requires prominent mention, a number of Dutch farmers left the Cape Colony in 1836, and, under the command of Pieter Retief, crossed the Drakensberg Mountains in 1837, and entered Natal. Their leader proceeded to Dingaan's capital, for the purpose of nego-

---

1. Strange to say, this Captain Allen Gardiner met the same cruel death some years afterwards, in South America.

tiating a treaty of peace and obtaining a formal cession of territory. In the last week of January, 1838, Pieter Retief, accompanied by seventy picked horsemen, crossed the Buffalo River, and on the 2nd of February arrived at Dingaan's *kraal*. The Zulu monarch fixed the 4th of February as the day for signing a formal cession of an immense district in Natal to the emigrant Boers.

The necessary document, drawn out by the Rev. Mr. Owen, missionary, with Dingaan, was duly signed, and business having been satisfactorily concluded, the Dutchmen were invited into the king's *kraal* to take leave of Dingaan. As requested, Retief and his followers left their arms outside. The Zulu monarch, surrounded by his favourite regiments, conversed in the most friendly manner, and while a "stirrup cup" of maize beer was in course of being drunk, suddenly cried out, "*Bulala matagati!*"—"Kill the wizards!" These words were the signal for a cruel massacre. More than 3000 savages beat to death, with *knobkerries*, the unfortunate Dutchmen who had been weak enough to trust to Zulu promises and Zulu honesty. The corpses of the slaughtered men were dragged out of the *kraal* to an adjacent hillock, and there allowed to become the prey of wolves and vultures.

Dingaan looked upon the massacre of the farmers who had vainly trusted to his honour as only a commencement of hostilities. Ten regiments were immediately ordered out to exterminate all the Dutch emigrants. While these people were, without suspicion, waiting for the return of their husbands and relatives, a Zulu army crawled up to their nearest camp, near the Blaauwkrantz River, close to the present commemorative town of Weenen, or "Weeping." A sudden surprise at the dawn of day was effected, and then ensued the barbarous murder in cold blood of every man, woman, and child.

Other detachments surprised other parties, and few escaped. The destroying army moved swiftly southward and towards the sea. Wherever the "*laager*" plan was adopted, it was successful; and at Necht Laager, on the Bushmans River, a few determined men succeeded in defending themselves against an overwhelming force of savages. The engagement lasted all day, but when the farmers' ammunition was nearly exhausted, the fire from an 8-pounder, rigged at the back of one of the wagons, killed several Zulu chiefs, and caused a precipitate retreat. The men who were afterwards able to visit the principal scenes of slaughter discovered frightful scenes of horror and misery. Wagons were demolished, and by their ruins lay the corpses of men, women, and children abandoned to the wild beasts.

Among the heaps of dead found at Weenen two young girls were picked out, one of whom had been pierced by nineteen *assegai* stabs, and the other by twenty-one. Both survived, although they remained cripples for life. It is estimated that in one week 600 white settlers were sacrificed as victims to the savage treachery of Dingaan.

Vengeance was determined upon by the Dutch emigrants, and a party of 400, having placed themselves under the command of Piet Uys and of Hendrik Potgieter, advanced from the Klip River Division against Dingaan. This took place in April, 1838; but unfortunately, shortly before, a party of Englishmen from D'Urban, with 700 friendly Zulus, having crossed the Tugela River near its mouth and destroyed a native town, the army of Dingaan, which had been kept in reserve, suddenly surrounded them and killed nearly every European.[2]

The conquerors followed up their success as far as D'Urban, and forced the few white people then resident there to take refuge on board a vessel named the *Comet*, fortunately lying at anchor in the bay. Dingaan, with his principal forces, watched the Dutch emigrants, and learned that Piet Uys and Hendrik Potgieter had placed themselves at the head of 400 men, with the object of invading Zululand. The wily savage allowed the Dutchmen to advance to a place closed in between two hills, within a few miles of his capital, and thence led them to a valley, where a desperate hand-to-hand combat took place. The farmers had been accustomed to fight by firing from horse- back, and then falling back rapidly to reload. They were so hemmed in by their position, that this mode of procedure was impossible, and they were at last, in desperation, compelled to concentrate their fire on one portion of the Zulu host. They then charged through the gap this made, and escaped. Unfortunately, Piet Uys did not succeed in cutting his way through, and died with his son, fighting bravely against terrible odds.

After this disastrous engagement, the Boers were so disheartened that hostilities were for some time suspended. They were renewed in August, 1838, when Dingaan attacked the Dutch in their *laagers*, but was in all cases repulsed with loss. Towards the close of that year, an army of 10,000 Zulus attacked the Dutch farmers in a strongly intrenched position at the Umslatoos River. The engagement took place on Sunday, the 16th of December. For three hours overwhelming masses of natives endeavoured to force the emigrant camp, until

---

2. The names of the principal Englishmen killed are—R. Biggar, Cane, Stubbs, Richard Wood, William Wood, Henry Batt, John Campbell, Thomas Campbell, and Thomas Carden.

Pretorius, finding that ammunition was beginning to fail, ordered 200 men to sally forth on horseback, and take the enemy in flank. This manoeuvre was successful, and the forces of Dingaan were compelled to fly, after leaving a large number on the field.[3]

After this decisive battle 6000 head of cattle were captured, and an advance was made to the hillock where lay the mortal remains of Retief and the brave men who perished with him. A frightful and ghastly spectacle was beheld: broken skulls, on which could be seen the marks of the *knobkerries* and stones with which they had been fractured, bones of legs and arms, and, strange to say, the skeleton of Retief, recognizable by a leathern pouch or *bandoleer*, in which was found the deed signed by Dingaan, resigning to the emigrant fanners "the place called Port Natal, together with all the land annexed; that is to say, from the Tugela to the Umzimvoboo River, and from the sea to the north, as far as the land may be useful and in my possession."

On the return of the emigrant Boers from this very successful attack on the Zulus, they were surprised to find that a small detachment of Highlanders, under the command of Major Charteris had taken possession of the Bay of Natal, This was done by order of Sir George Napier, Governor of the Cape Colony, from a desire[4] "to put an end to the unwarranted occupation of parts of the territories belonging to the natives by certain emigrants of the Cape Colony, being subjects of his Majesty." No conflict, however, took place at this time. The Dutch were busily employed during the year 1839 in laying out the towns of Pietermaritzborg [5] and D'Urban, as well as in appointing *landrosts* or magistrates, and establishing regulations for the government of the country. Dingaan frequently sent in ambassadors charged with messages of peace, but it was soon discovered that this was merely a plan for carrying out a system of espionage.

A brother of Dingaan, named Panda, who had been generally looked upon with contempt as a mere sensualist who was undisposed for the fatigues of warfare, became an object of jealousy to the king, in consequence of a large party among the Zulus, who were tired of constant fighting and bloodshed, showing some disposition to prefer him to his brother. An attempt to capture and kill Panda was followed by his flight across the Tugela into Natal, and his application to the Dutch emigrant farmers for assistance. Such an opportunity was glad-

---

3. The Dutch Bay 3000 Zulus were killed; but this is probably a great exaggeration.
4. Proclamation in the Government *Gazette*.
5. Called after a Dutchman named Pieter Maritz.

ly seized upon; and in the next year (1840) an army of Panda's, 4000 strong, was joined by 400 mounted farmers, under the command of Andries Pretorius. While the forces were mustering in Pietermaritzb-nrg, an ambassador from Dingaan, named Tamboosa, arrived, bringing proposals for peace. Upon being seized and questioned, this messenger admitted that one of the objects of his mission was to obtain every possible information, with a view of reporting it to his master.

This, however, by no means justified the blunder and crime com-mitted by the Dutch farmers, who put Tamboosa to death, and would not even listen to his prayer for mercy on behalf of his young attend-ant, who suffered with him. Scarcely was this execution over when the armies of Dingaan and Panda met in battle. In this fierce encounter two regiments were entirely destroyed, and the fortune of the day declared in favour of Panda, merely in consequence of a portion of his brother's army deserting in his favour. The Dutch farmers vigorously followed up this success, and forced Dingaan to take shelter among a small tribe close to Delagoa Bay, who killed him in order to secure the favour of his conquerors.

On the 14th of February, 1840, and on the banks of the Umvolosi River, the emigrant Boers proclaimed Panda king of the Zulu people, and at the same time declared that their own sovereignty extended from St. Lucia Bay to the Umzimvoboo (St. John's). Shortly previous to this date, Sir George Napier had ordered the British garrison to abandon D'Urban, and Captain Jervis, who held the local command, said, on the occasion of his departure, that he wished the inhabitants peace and happiness, hoping that they would cultivate these beauti-ful regions in quiet and prosperity, "ever regardful of the rights of the people whose country you have adopted, and whose home you have made your own.

We cannot be surprised that, under all the circumstances, the emi-grant Boers looked upon Natal as rightfully their country, and that the British Government had even abandoned it in their favour. Having assisted in conquering Dingaan, and placed Panda upon the throne, there was no reason to fear native aggressions. No fewer than 36,000 head of cattle were given in by the new monarch as an indemnity, so that the Boers were able to settle down not only in peace, but with considerable additional means at their disposal.

The government adopted by this society of farmers was of an ex-ceedingly ill-concerted character, and soon proved to be essentially anarchic and unworkable. The legislative, executive, and judicial powers were centred in a Volksraad of twenty-four members, who were required to assemble every three months at Pietermaritzburg. All the members performed their duties gratuitously, but *landrosts*, each of whom enjoyed a salary of £100 *per annum*, were appointed at the chief town, as well as at D'Urban and Weenen. Two or three members of the Volksraad, who happened to live near Pietermaritzburg, formed what was styled the Commissie Raad, to whom executive functions requiring immediate despatch were entrusted; but whatever they did had to be submitted for approval to the entire Volksraad.

Besides, a federal bond of union existed with the Winunrg, Caledon, and Madder districts of the Orange Free State, from which places, delegates were sent. The acts of the Commissie Raad, as well as those of the permanent officials, were so assailed in the Volksraad, and such personal and offensive attacks were indulged in by this body, that good government became impossible; and so little was law respected, that Judge Cloete informs us that when he arrived as Commissioner in 1848, the *landrost* of Pietermaritzburg informed him that a judgment which he had passed several months before, against a respectable inhabitant living only a few miles from that town, ordering him to return cattle which he had illegally withheld from a Hottentot, was still a dead letter, as the defendant had openly declared he would shoot the first messenger of the law who should dare to come on his premises.

The Volksraad of the Boers had applied to the Governor of the Cape Colony for acknowledgment and recognition of the State as free and independent, and Sir George Napier had returned an answer by no means unfavourable, but their conduct soon made it evident that it would be impossible to grant their petition. Stock was stolen from Natal farmers towards the end of the year 1840, and armed *burghers*, under Andries Pretorius, were instructed to pursue the thieves. Traces of cattle, supposed to be those stolen, were followed to some *kraals* of the Amabaka tribe, and without any delay these people were attacked, several killed, 8000 head of cattle and 250 sheep and goats carried off. At the same time seventeen children were seized—in fact, captured as slaves.

The conduct of Pretorius was approved by the Volksraad, but Sir George Napier found himself obliged to reprobate it in the strongest language. British troops were immediately sent to the Umgasi River, between the Kei and the Umzimvoboo, and His Excellency declined any further intercourse with the emigrant Boers, unless they distinctly acknowledged that they were subjects of the Queen of England. Although the Home Government was at that time very reluctant to extend its colonial possessions, a despatch was sent to Sir George Napier, in which he was informed that her Majesty could not acknowledge the independence of her own subjects, but that the trade of the emigrant Boers would be placed upon the same footing as that of any other British settlement, upon their receiving a military force to exclude the interference with the country by any other European power.

It was then within the option of the Boers to secure all the substantial advantages of self government; but as in the Transvaal now, so in Natal at the period in question—obstinate folly animated the councils of the people, and an ultimatum was sent, stating their intention "to remain on the same footing as heretofore." Upon this, Sir George Napier issued a proclamation, in which it was stated that as the emigrant farmers had refused to be recognised or treated as British subjects, and had recently passed a resolution by which all Kafirs inhabiting Natal were to be removed, without their consent, into the country of Faku (Pondoland), military occupation of the colony would be resumed. Shortly afterwards, the troops stationed at the Umgazi camp were ordered to march to Natal. This small force, consisting of 250 men, besides a small party of the Cape corps and two field-pieces, arrived safely at D'Urban, and a few days afterwards the brig *Pilot* came to anchor in the bay, bringing them stores and provisions, as well as two 18-pounders and ammunition. This vessel was soon afterwards followed by the schooner *Mazeppa*.

The Volksraad of the emigrant Boers was astonished and indignant at the military occupation of D'Urban, and more than 300 men, under Andries Pretorius, were immediately ordered out. The capture of some cattle, and the receipt of a letter ordering him to quit Natal, so enraged the commander of the small English force, that he led a night attack against the Dutch camp at Congella. So ill managed, however, was the expedition, that Captain Smith was repulsed and his guns captured. Out of 140 men whom he led in this unfortunate affray no fewer than 103 were killed, wounded, and missing. He then saw that his little force was reduced to extremities, but exerted himself most indefatigably and perseveringly to resist to the last.

A fortification something similar in character to a *laager* was formed at D'Urban, by means of the numerous wagons in the camp, with the requisite trenches and mounds. The Dutch Boers fortunately allowed the time in which they should have taken advantage of their victory to pass by, and soon saw that, in consequence of their inertness, a conquest which in the first instance would have been easy was now converted into a siege. In the meantime Captain Smith was able to send off for assistance to the Cape Colony. Richard King, then living in a hut at D'Urban, volunteered to carry the despatches. Mr. G. C. Cato conveyed him and his horses across the channel to the Bluff, and then he rode off, leading a spare horse, and before daybreak succeeded in passing the Umcomas River. There he was safe from the danger of pursuit, but had to face the perils of crossing two hundred rivers, and of traversing a wild country inhabited by savages. Upon this slender thread hung the destinies of the British in Natal.

Encouraged by their success, the Boers overpowered the detachment of British troops stationed at the Point, and took most of the English residents prisoners to Pietermaritzburg.[6] Then all their efforts were directed against the fort, in which Captain Smith had been able to mount an 18-pounder and to secure provisions and ammunition. The farmers, who had three field-pieces, carried on a heavy cannonade for three days, and when they had exhausted their ammunition, turned the siege into a rigorous blockade. Two sorties made by the garrison were unavailing, and at last the rations were reduced to the smallest quantity sufficient to sustain life; dried horseflesh became the principal article of food, and the utmost anxiety prevailed as to the success of Richard King, and the arrival of reinforcements from the Cape Colony. Many a time eyes were strained for some sign of assistance; at last, on the night of the 24th of June, they saw, with inexpressible relief, the rockets and blue lights which announced that a vessel with reinforcements had arrived.

Dick King had succeeded. After a ride of many hundreds of miles over trackless, unknown, and savage regions, he had safely reached the Cape Colony. It was on the ninth day after he left the Bluff at Natal that he arrived, almost exhausted, in Graham's Town. Colonel Hare, the Lieutenant-Governor of the Eastern Province, immediately sent the grenadier company of the 27th Regiment, in the schooner *Conch*, from Port Elizabeth, and when Sir George Napier heard the news in Cape Town, he lost no time in persuading Admiral Percy to despatch the flagship *Southampton*, with the 25th Regiment on board, under

6. A little vessel, the *Mazeppa*, Captain Cato, escaped from the inner harbour, although fired upon by the Boers, and proceeded to Delagoa Bay in order to obtain assistance. She found no British man-of-war there, and on her return to Natal H.H.S. *Southampton* had arrived.

the command of Colonel Cloete. The ship of war arrived at Natal only one day after the *Conch*. A landing was immediately effected with very trifling lose; the Boer force was driven back to the Congella. A gale of wind drove the *Southampton* to sea, and supplies became so scarce that Colonel Cloete was obliged to obtain the services of Zulus to secure cattle. Some of these killed two Dutch farmers, and this gave occasion to a panic among the Boers, who precipately fled to Pietermaritzburg.

Amidst great consternation and great confusion, a meeting of the Volksraad was held in the church at Pietermaritzburg, when recriminations, quarrelling, and loud talking occupied the entire Sunday. At last it was resolved to propose terms of peace to Colonel Cloete; but the ignorance and simplicity of the Boers were displayed by their holding out as a threat the succour they might receive from the King of Holland, to whom letters had some time previously been sent by the hands of a trader named Smellekamp. After negotiations. Colonel Cloete granted an amnesty to all except four ringleaders, and Natal was peaceably once more under the rule of the British Crown.

These transactions took place in 1842; and in the following year the Honourable Henry Cloete, afterwards a Judge of the Supreme Court of the Cape Colony, was sent to Natal as her Majesty's Commissioner, with ample authority to inaugurate a settled system of government, and to put an end to the anarchy and confusion which prevailed. By the exercise of great tact and judgment he was successful. A powerful radical faction in the Volksraad opposed submission in the most outrageous and foolish manner. They even adopted a plan to assassinate the leading members of the peace party; but Andries Pretorius, one of the latter, and a wise, true friend of his adopted country, having discovered the plot, exposed it publicly, and brought its authors to shame.

Judge Cloete tells us that this patriot addressed the meeting in a strain of impassioned extemporaneous eloquence not unworthy of Cicero when denouncing Cataline, and turned the tide so powerfully against the would-be assassins as to entirely defeat their plot. Entire submission to the British Government followed. Major Smith was succeeded by Colonel Boys, of the 45th Regiment, as military commandant, and his Honour Martin West, resident magistrate of Graham's Town, was appointed the first Lieutenant-Governor of Natal.

Chapter 2

Native Policy in Natal

The protection of the natives was the professed object of the British Government in taking possession of Natal. The conquests of Chaka had driven no fewer than 100,000 fugitives to the westward of the Tugela River, and how to rule this vast and fast increasing number of natives soon became a problem fraught both with difficulty and danger. Mr. Theophilus Shepstone, son of a Wesleyan missionary, thoroughly conversant with the Kafir language, customs, manners, and habits, was appointed to take charge of the numerous natives of Natal. His policy can be very briefly described. It was to keep all the coloured races entirely distinct from the white population. They were collected in locations, and governed by their own laws, through their own chiefs, under Mr. Shepstone as the great chief.

Large tracts of country, rugged and mountainous, were set apart for the various tribes, and there, in an Italian climate, and in the lap of a most productive and generous soil, they increased and multiplied. Christianity and real civilization were ignored, and a most dangerous *imperium in imperio* created. The wretched refugees who fled from the Zulu tyrant found their lot in Natal incomparably more happy than in the precarious existence of former days. Their easy, savage, sensuous life made them useless citizens, and when labour was required for the sugar plantations on the coast, it had to be obtained from India.

However smoothly and well the native policy seemed to work, it soon became very evident that the 20,000 white people of Natal were really seated on a political volcano. Three hundred thousand heathen savages of an alien race had the power to rise and destroy them at any moment, and it was impossible to be sure that they might not at any time have the inclination. All the checks which religion and civilization place on men had been deliberately cast aside. No doubt the Zulu monarch was feared; but there can be no doubt also that if the dread paramount ruler of the Zulu race had at any time crossed the Tugela as s conqueror, tens of thousands of his own race in the colony would have joined him out of fear, and hastened to prove their loyalty by the massacre of every white inhabitant of Natal. This is no fanciful idea, but sober earnest fact.[1]

There was no difficulty at first in subjecting to proper control the broken, dispirited hands of refugees, who sought shelter, food, and protection in Natal; and if right methods had been adopted, one of the finest races of the African continent would have been raised from a state of loathsome degradation to one of civilization—saved from heathenism themselves to become coadjutors with the white races in raising the country to real prosperity. In place of this, the cruel slavery of polygamy was permitted, which allows the men to live in independent idleness by means of the severe drudgery of their oppressed wives. Grossly impure and inhuman laws and practices, including the vile superstitions of witchcraft, were tolerated and allowed.

No country could advance under such circumstances, and the colony of Natal, therefore, remains at the present day what it has always been—immeasurably behind the Cape of Good Hope; a land of samples in which nothing really succeeds, and where sugar, which forms its principal export, is even now a doubtful experiment, on which labour imported from India at enormous cost has to be employed; a lovely country, whose fertility is almost as great as its beauty, but cursed by a most unchristian, wicked, and foolish system of government, so far as the great bulk of the population is concerned. It would have been very easy at the outset to establish comparatively small locations, presided over by British magistrates, who would have administered justice according to British law.

If, in addition, title-deeds had been given in such a manner as to give individual rights, then, in the words of the Rev. W. C. Holden,[2] the large number of natives within the colony might have been converted into men who would take a real interest in the country and soil, for the defence of which they would fight and die. They would have become a strong wall of defence against the Zulu on the east,

---

1. The writer has been assured of this by old inhabitants, who spoke the Zulu tongue like natives, and had been brought up with Zulu refugees. There is no doubt whatever that if Cetywayo had entered Natal with a large victorious army, one of the most awful massacres on record would have been the result.
2. *History of the Colony of Natal*, p. 205.

and the Amaxosa on the west, instead of a source of continual danger and alarm.[3] Slavery was abolished everywhere throughout the British dominions, with the one exception of Natal. There 50,000 women were sold for wives to the highest bidder, as horses, cattle, and goods at an auction mart, under the special sanction and special arrangement of the Queen's Government.

Before proceeding farther, it is necessary to pass briefly in review the laws, manners, and customs of the Zulu race. Without a knowledge of this subject it will he perfectly impossible to appreciate the policy of Sir Bartle Frere, or to understand either the real causes of the war, or of many events in its progress. We have seen that Chaka, the Zulu conqueror, formed a great military nation. His successors were specially warriors, and as the people chose similar weapons to those with which the ancient Romans conquered the world, so, like that people, were they fully animated with the feeling that *virtus*, or the highest possible merit, consisted in bravery in the field of battle.

The Boers despised the enemy, and hundreds of their bravest men fell victims. Almost about the same time, the English settlers at D'Urban made the same mistake, and 2000 of their Kafir allies, as well as several of their own number, were slaughtered and left to be devoured by beasts of prey on the hills of Zululand. History repeats itself: Lord Chelmsford made the same mistake, which was expiated in the blood of hundreds of British soldiers on the field of Isandhlwana.

Among the Zulus every female child is so much property, and in this respect treated exactly like a chattel or beast of burden. Her life is one of the grossest degradation and slavery. When she has reached the age of puberty disgusting ceremonies are performed, and there is no idea or appreciation of chastity. The most brutal lust is not only tolerated, but actually enforced by law. When a girl is married, she is merely sold to the highest bidder, entirely without reference to her own consent, and then becomes the slave of her husband, for whom she has to labour in the field and perform menial work.

The day after the party of a bride has arrived at her owner's hut, the peculiar ceremony takes place of the woman being allowed and

3. Sir George Grey, writing many years ago, tells us of the Maoris in New Zealand, that nearly the whole nation has now been converted to Christianity; that they are fond of agriculture; take great pleasure in cattle and horses; like the sea, and form good sailors, have now many coasting vessels of their own; are attached to Europeans, and admire their customs and manners; and that they are extremely ambitions of rising in civilization, and becoming skilled in European arts.

enjoined to tax her powers to the utmost to use abusive language to her lord. She pours every insulting and provoking epithet she can think of upon him, this being the last time in which she is permitted to act and speak independently. At last she takes a certain feather out of her head, by means of which the act of marriage, or rather of going into slavery, becomes complete. Mr. Holden speaks of the great obscenity at "marriage" celebrations, and remarks that "no respectable pages can be defiled with a description of what then takes place, especially in connection with the marriage of men of rank and chiefs. There is full licence given to wholesale debauchery, and both men and women glory in their shame."[4]

It is impossible to pursue this subject further. This is certain, that the very grossest and most filthy obscenities and immoralities are absolutely enjoined and required by Zulu law and custom. Marriage is entirely a misnomer. To quote from an excellent authority, "No word corresponding to the Saxon word 'wife' is found in the Zulu language. The term most nearly approaching to it is *umkake*, and its correlatives *umkako* and *umkami*, which means his *she* or *female*. The man owns his wives as truly, according to native law, as he does his spear or his goat, and he speaks of them accordingly."

The owner of the woman says, "I have paid so many cattle for you; therefore you are *my slave*, my dog, and your proper place is under my feet." One of these poor slaves, when seen standing by a load far too great for her strength, was asked if she could carry it. She stood up and ingenuously remarked, "If I were a man I could not, but I am a woman." There is no slavery in the world more sad or deplorable than that to which the poor women of the Zulu nation are subjected.[5]

Spiritualism is the religion of the Zulu, and witchcraft is the machinery by means of which it is practised. Only a very vague idea exists about a Supreme Being, and the definite national faith embraces only a belief in the influence of the spirits of deceased ancestors. The ghosts of departed chiefs and warriors are specially respected and feared. It is to these spirits that they attribute all the power given by Christians to God, and the witchdoctors are the mediums or priests of the worship, A knowledge of subtle and powerful vegetable poisons exists, and so

---

4. *The Past and Future of the Kafir Races*, p. 198.
5. The common price of a wife is from ten to twelve head of cattle, but a strong and young woman of good muscular frame often commands as many as fifty oxen. When the sale is completed, the woman must go into slavery, and, if she run away, is frequently hunted for with dogs.

common is the practice of secret poisoning that universal safeguards are used against it.

Everyone who gives food to another takes a part himself, in proof that it contains no poison. Besides deadly drugs, there is what is styled the "*ubuti*," or bewitching matter, which is supposed to be deposited in some secret place, and to be made the instrument of evil by means of supernatural agency. The "*isanusi*," or witchdoctors, are the go-betweens, whose duty it is to discover and to avert evil. These men fill the threefold office of doctors, priests, and soothsayers. They heal diseases, offer sacrifices, and exercise the art of divination. As they are assumed to have full power over the invisible world, their influence is enormous, and is readily taken advantage of by chiefs and powerful men, for the purpose of destroying enemies and promoting schemes of war and plunder.

A youth who aspires to be enrolled among the *isanusi* gives early signs of being destined for the office. He dreams of the spirits of the departed chiefs of his people, sees visions, falls into fits of frenzy; he catches snakes and twists them round his person, seeks out medicinal roots, and goes for instruction to experienced *isanasi*. At last what is called a "change in the moon" takes place within him; he becomes a medium fitted to hold converse with spirits, and is able to communicate with them. One of the greatest authorities who has ever lived with and studied the Kafir races—Mr. Warner—says:

"It is impossible to suppose that these priests are not, to a considerable extent, self-deceived, as well as the deceivers of others; and there is no difficulty, to one who believes the Bible to be a divine revelation, in supposing that they are also to a certain extent under Satanic influence; for the idolatrous and heathen nations of the earth are declared in the inspired volume to be, in a peculiar manner, under the influence and power of the devil."

Every illness and misfortune is supposed to be caused by witchcraft. It usually happens that the suspected person is a rich man, or someone on whom it is thought desirable to wreak vengeance. The people of the *kraal* and neighbourhood go in a body to the *isanusi*, who, before their arrival, foretells their approach, and makes other revelations, frequently so extraordinary that the Rev. Mr. Holden,[6] who is thoroughly conversant with the subject, states that there is much greater difficulty in explaining these phenomena by ordinary means than by supernatural interposition. The whole company, on arrival,

---

6. *Kafir Races*, p. 287.

sit down and salute the witchdoctor; they are then told to beat the ground with their sticks, and while this is in course of being done, he repeatedly shouts out, "*Yeswa!*"—"He is here!"

He discloses secrets about the accused, and at last, fixing his eyes upon the doomed one, charges him with the crime. Generally the *isanusi* succeeds in selecting the suspected person; but if he fail, a circle is formed, and a wild, frenzied dance performed, amidst most frightful gesticulations and cries. Among the Zulus, not only is the unfortunate person killed whom the witchdoctor declares guilty, but his wife and children are murdered, and his property seized. Among the Amaxosa Kafirs, the most frightful tortures are used to induce the unfortunate victim to confess.[7] It is difficult to appreciate adequately the enormous power of the witchdoctors. It was in 1857 that Umhlakaza was made a willing tool in the hands of Kreli, Sandilli, and Umhala for the purpose of a war of extermination against the whites.

It was prophesied that if the people destroyed their cattle and corn, the whole would rise again with vast increase, and that their enemies would be utterly destroyed. Sir George Grey had taken every precaution, and war was therefore made impossible. Like the witches in *Macbeth*, the prophet had merely lured on his victims to destruction. Having burned their ships, by destroying all their resources there was no escape, and, in spite of the humane exertions of the colonists, 70,000 human beings perished of famine in a land of plenty. It will thus be seen how an entire people can easily be induced to embark in the most desperate undertakings by the skilful use of the superstitious means at the disposal of their chiefs. Sacrifices of beasts are offered by the priests, according to prescribed roles. These are made to the spirits of the departed.

A hut is sacredly cleaned and set apart, in which the sacrifice is shut up during the night, in order that the "*isituta*," or spirits, may drink in its flavour. On the next day the place is opened, and the meat de-

---

7. The Hon. Mr. Godlonton, in his *Case for the Colonists*, gives us details of one of the very numerous cases of torture inflicted on men whose only guilt was their wealth, and who fell victims to the avarice of their tor mentors. Although this poor victim implored for death, it was not granted to him until he had been literally roasted. Red-hot stones were placed on his groin, and when they slipped off, were held in position by means of sticks. Another very common torture is that of smearing a victim, and then allowing him to be slowly eaten up by black ants or scorpions, whose thousand bites and stings produce lingering and excruciating torture. All these infernal proceedings take place in connection with the spiritualist religion, and are carried out by the order and direction of its priests.

voured by the people. All sacrifices, with trifling exceptions, must be offered by priests. The blood is never spilt, but caught in a vessel, and it is necessary to burn the bones. The frenzy or inspired madness characteristic of the priests of the ancient oracles is commonly assumed by the priests of the Zulu spiritualists, and many of their ceremonies are occult, and have never been made known to Europeans.

The Zulu government is thoroughly despotic. The will of the tyrant is law, and he has unlimited power of life or death. We have seen that Chaka sacrificed everything to military power, and in order to succeed, banished even circumcision, and refused to allow his warriors to marry. Women's love and children's tenderness were forbidden to the stern soldiers of the new empire. Medicines composed of various plants and roots were used to purify the body and make it strong, and ordinarily sacrifices were offered for the same purpose. The great national sacrifice to make the army invulnerable is styled "*ukokofula,*" when flesh is cut off the shoulder of a living beast and roasted on a fire into which certain charms have been thrown.

Each man bites off a mouthful, and passes on the meat to the next, while the priest makes incisions in parts of their bodies, into which he inserts the powdered charcoal of the charms. The poor animal is left in torture all this time, and is not killed until the ceremonies are ended. A decoction is also prepared from medicinal roots, and sprinkled by means of the tail of an ox over the bodies of the warriors. All this is designed to make the Zulus either invulnerable, or to enable them, if they do fall in battle, to join triumphantly the heroes of their race in the spirit world. The three great divisions of the army already referred to, comprising "men," "young men," and "carriers," were sub-divided into regiments with a proper staff of officers.

The Zulu strength is in attack, when with ferocious yells they throw themselves with undaunted bravery upon their enemy. Two horns advance and endeavour to flank the foe, while the main body follows quickly to their support. *Virtus*—military bravery—is their *summum bonum,* and death is the immediate penalty of any form of cowardice. Extreme cunning and dissimulation are considered essential qualifications of a general, so that to lure a foe into ambush, or to deceive him by illusory promises or messages of peace, are considered proofs of wisdom and ability. Honour, humanity, and generosity are perfectly unknown, and merely considered signs of weakness.

When an enemy is defeated, prisoners are never taken, and those not killed in the heat of battle are cruelly tortured and mutilated, with every mark of indignity and contempt. Women and children are not spared, and the most cruel destruction of the most cruel northern barbarians, who devastated Europe, pales before the complete and effectual ruin which marks the progress of a Zulu conqueror.

In times of peace the army remains at military *kraals*, and is occasionally called up to the great place of the king for review. It is always in a state of readiness, and burning for employment. War is the pastime, glory, and wish of the men, who eagerly desire to wash their spears in blood, that they may obtain the only glory for which they care to live, and secure that plunder which can enable them to acquire wives and cattle. Nothing could be more dangerous, or a more awful threat to a colony, than an army of this description under the orders of a despotic savage, without the slightest principle, and urged on to fight by all the traditions and ideas of his race.

Let it be remembered also that the country of Natal was once owned by the Zulus, and that, while held by a garrison of only 20,000 whites, there were no fewer than 300,000 savage heathen inhabitants in it of similar colour, race, and religion to the people of Cetywayo. Once let the flood-gates be lifted and a conquering "invulnerable" army enter Natal, nothing could prevent the general rising of the vast masses of natives within that colony. If that had occurred, British dominion would have set in an ocean of blood, and every white man, woman, and child in the settlement must have been slaughtered. It was one wise, good man who averted that catastrophe, and his name was Bartle Frere. Slowly, but most certainly, will the mists of prejudice be lifted from the minds of the English people, and they will learn to know that the policy they so much vilified saved the British name from dishonour, and the British people and British interests in South Africa from destruction.

CHAPTER 3

Commencement of Hostilities

Thirty-six years had elapsed since the eventful ride of Dick King from D'Urban to Graham's Town. The British colony of Natal had grown slowly. Immigrants arrived; a representative Constitution was granted. During this period numbers of people of Dutch extraction formed settlements in the Orange Free State and Transvaal Republic. The British Government in the first instance established sovereignty over the former country, but abandoned it on the 23rd of February, 1854. The Republic commenced from that date. So far as the Transvaal is concerned, Potgieter established the town of Potchefstroom in 1839, and soon after enormous territory, extending from the Vaal to the Limpopo, came under the dominion of the South African Republic.

The first session of *Volksraad* was held in 1848, and it was in 1862 that Pretorius succeeded in obtaining the treaty at Sand River, by means of which the independence of the Republic was recognized by the British Crown. One of the first Acts of the Volksraad was to repeal a former resolution fixing their southern boundary at the twenty-fifth degree of south latitude, because the Volksraad has no means of determining where the said degree of south latitude is. Amongst the people civilization made slow progress.

"Not many years ago," wrote Mr. Thomas Baines in his valuable work on the *Gold Regions of South Eastern Africa*, "their own surveyor general was mobbed for using a theodolite in the streets of Potchefstroom instead of stepping off the distance like the *Veld-Valkt meester* of the good old times."

Sir Arthur Cunynhame, in his recent narrative, gives us yet more amusing and stirling illustrations of the utter simplicity and ignorance of the Boers. As was to be expected under the circumstances, the

Government was extremely narrow and objectionable; in proof of which it is only necessary to state that no Englishman or German was allowed to possess landed property, it was forbidden to discover or work minerals, while slavery really existed, and was practised under what was styled the Apprentice Law, passed in 1856.[1] In spite of the discovery of goldfields

At Pilgrim's Rest., the country became insolvent, wars with the natives took place, and at last such a state of insolvency and danger was attained that the British Government found it imperatively necessary to intervene. The Zulus under Cetywayo, intended to overrun the country, and this would have threatened all British South Africa. The northern territory of the State had already been abandoned to the natives; the Government was powerless, and all confidence in it had fled; commerce was destroyed, and the country was bankrupt. Under these circumstances. Sir Theophilus Shepstone, on the 12th of April, 1877, found himself imperatively obliged to place the Transvaal territory under the protection of the British flag.

In Natal, under the administration of Sir Benjamin Pine, during the year 1873, a rebellion broke out on the part of a chief named Langalibalele, which was only prevented from becoming a general war by the admirably prompt action of the local Government. The philanthropic societies in England, with Bishop Colenso, championed the cause of this rebel, and Sir B. Pine was, in consequence of their exertions, recalled. Sir Garnet Wolseley, who succeeded that officer, says, "Langalibalele, as I am informed by all classes here, official and non-official (a small knot of men of extreme views excepted), is regarded by the native population at large as a chief who, having defied the authorities, and in doing so occasioned the murder of two white men, is now suffering for that conduct. In their opinion his attempts to brave the Government have been checkmated, and his banishment from the colony, regarded as a lenient punishment by the natives at large, cannot fail to be a serious warning to all other Kafir chiefs, not only in Natal but in the whole of South Africa, to avoid imitating his example."[2]

Sir Garnet Wolseley effected an important change in the colonial legislature, by adding eight nominee members to the Council, which

---

1. For proof of these charges see *Jeppe-Transvaal Book Almanack for 1879.* Gideon Steyn, who reported the existence of slavery to Sir P. E. Wodehouse in 1869, was fired at in Potchefstroom.
2. Sir Garnet Wolseley, quoted in the *Contemporary Review,* June, 1879.

previously consisted of five *ex-officio* and fifteen elected members. The annexation of the Transvaal followed; and, speaking of this, Sir Benjamin Pine says that "the strong ground taken in defence of the measure is that its hostilities with the native tribes seriously imperilled the peace of our colonies—that it was, in fact, a next-door neighbour's house in flames, which might any moment set ours on fire. In this respect, the ground for annexing the Transvaal Republic was very much stronger than that which justified our taking possession of Natal. The latter country did not at that time touch our boundary at any point. It was a house several streets off."

The discovery of diamonds in South Africa, in 1867, exercised by degrees an enormous influence upon the attitude of the natives throughout Southern Africa. When the success of the dry diggings at the New Bush caused the formation of Kimberley, that town became the centre of an enormous gun trade. From north and east, thousands of Kafirs of various tribes flocked to a place where they could obtain, for the reward of their labour, the means of exterminating the hated white man in South Africa. The Gealekas under Kreli, the Gaikas of Sandilli, as well as the Zulus beyond Natal, were not slow to seize such an opportunity. For years the trade continued, and the weapons purchased were soon used against the Government which permitted their sale.

Wars were waged upon the eastern and northern borders of the Cape Colony during 1877, 1878, and 1879. Sir Benjamin Pine, with some fancy and a great deal of truth, styles the diamond of the Kimberley mines the bloodstone of South Africa. As the Zulu system makes war a necessity constantly thirsted for by the army, advantage was taken of the easy opportunity of getting firearms afforded by the inconceivable blindness and fatuity of the British Government. In the year 1877, Cetywayo had quite made up his mind for a deadly conflict with the white man. Guns were purchased, preparations were made, and the army crouched like a tiger in its lair, ready to spring.

Since the first establishment of the colony of Natal, and of the Transvaal Republic, the Governments of these countries had the Zulu military power suspended, like the sword of Damocles, as a perpetual threat over their heads. Of course, by the annexation of the latter State in 1877, all its responsibilities devolved upon Her Majesty's Government. Cetywayo, the son of Panda, succeeded his father in the year 1872, and it formed part of Sir T. Shepstone's policy to conciliate and please him in every possible manner. That officer went so far as to attend his coronation, which was celebrated with the grandest forms of savage ceremonial.[3]

At the same time a number of promises and engagements were received from the king. All this was, of course, merely a solemn farce. The descendant of Dingaan, who first signed a deed giving Natal to the Dutch, and then murdered in cold blood the men who had trusted to his honour, was not likely to depart from the traditions and policy of his race. Dissimulation, fraud, and cunning . are characteristic qualities of every Zulu ruler, and Cetywayo excelled in them all. The Government of Natal was lulled into security, while Bishop Colenso and the well-meaning but profoundly ignorant men who form the self-styled philanthropical societies in England have, even up to the present moment, been completely hoodwinked and deceived.

Sir Bartle Frere, writing of Cetywayo's solemn promises, says, "None of these promises have been since fulfilled; the cruelties and barbarisms which deformed the internal administration of Zululand in Panda's reign have been aggravated during the reign of Cetywayo, and his relations with his neighbours have been conducted in a spirit fatal to peace and security beyond the Zulu border." [4]

The well-organized and peculiarly formidable military power of the Zulus was still further consolidated and strengthened by Cetywayo, so that a standing menace and threat of a very serious nature existed against both Natal and the Transvaal. Nothing can better prove the danger than the fact that the Zulu monarch formally and repeatedly requested the consent of the British Government to wars of aggression, which he proposed for the ostensible purpose of initiating his young soldiers in bloodshed, and reviving the system of unprovoked territorial aggression which had been so successfully carried out by the model and demi-god of the nation—Chaka.

A large tract of land on the western boundary of Zululand, between the Buffalo and Pongolo Rivers, which had long formed part of the Transvaal, was claimed by the Zulus, and they had requested the Natal Government to arbitrate in this matter. Eventually a Commission was appointed, which decided that Cetywayo's cession of a tract of land relied on by the Transvaal claim was promised when he was only heir apparent, and that the cession had not been subsequently formally ratified by his father Panda, nor by the great council of the

---

3. For a description of this ceremony, see Baines's *South Africa*. This traveller was present on the occasion.

4. Memorandum by his Excellency the High Commissioner, January, 1878.

Zulu nation; therefore the country in question had never ceased to belong to them. Private rights of *bonâ fide* settlers, which could not in justice be abrogated, were confirmed, but otherwise the sovereignty of the territory was ceded to the Zulus.

Since his installation the tone of Cetywayo had become entirely altered. When a remonstrance was sent against a barbarous murder of young women by the king, replies of extreme insolence were sent to the Natal Government, and the opportunity was taken to state that no responsibility was admitted; at the same time, the solemn installation promises were distinctly denied, and Cetywayo affirmed his intention of shedding blood in future on a much greater scale. In the latter part of July, 1878, the Zulu chief Sirayo entered British territory, carried off two women—British subjects—and forcibly put them to death. Redress was demanded, but not given.

On the 11th of December, 1878, a final message was sent to Cetywayo, in which the reasonable and just demands of the Government were summarized. He was called upon to give up the offenders who had violated British territory, and to effect various reforms in the administration of his government, in accordance with the solemn promises made at his installation. A few informal messages made and retracted only served to show the cunning and deceit of Cetywayo, and it was clear to demonstration that the Zulu potentate and the Zulu army had determined upon war.

The High Commissioner writes (30th September) to the Imperial Government:—

It is difficult to give any adequate idea of the strength of evidence of the state of feeling. Zulu regiments are reported as moving about on unusual and special errands, several of them organizing royal hunts on a great scale in parts of the country where little game is to be expected, and where the obvious object is to guard the border against attack. The hunters are said to have received orders to follow any game they may rouse across the border, which it appears is, according to Zulu custom, a recognized mode of provoking or declaring war.

Unusual bodies of armed men are stated to watch all drifts and roads leading into Zululand, and these guards are occasionally reported as warning off Natal natives from entering the Zulu territory, accompanying the warning with contemptuous intimation that orders have been given to kill all Natalions if they trespass across the border. Zulu subjects came hastily into Natal to reclaim cattle which they had sent hither to graze, giving as their reason that Zululand is so disturbed that they know not what will happen. Serious alarm is expressed because three large ships have been seen on the coast making for Delagoa Bay, and great irritation is expressed by Zulus at the stoppage of the supplies of arms and ammunition they used to receive through that port.

The reports first received of raids into Natal territory by large bodies of armed men, who dragged two refugee women out of the huts of British subjects, with expressions of contemptuous disregard for what the English Government might think, or say, or do, and the murder of the women directly they were on the other side of the boundary line, appear to be confirmed in every particular.

There seems to be no doubt that the parties were headed by two sons of Sirayo. This chief lives near the Natal border, and was well known as extremely anti-English in his feelings. Until quite lately he was so little in favour with Cetywayo, that he had not for some time attended to any summons to the royal kraal. He was nevertheless appointed by Cetywayo to represent him at the Boundary Commission.

Partly, it was said, on account of his rank and influence and known antipathy to Europeans, and partly because he could not refuse to attend at the royal kraal to give an account of his stewardship, he did so attend, and in the absence of the prime minister, was appointed to act for him, a proceeding which, considering his known anti-English feeling, is regarded as significant.

It is to be remembered that the facts, of which a brief summary is here given, have been sifted from. a mass of very alarming rumours, current during the month, which His Excellency the Lieutenant-Governor considered more doubtful, or unworthy of credit, but which are circulated in a manner to increase agitation and excitement on both sides of the border.

The only question remained—Were we to allow the enemy to wait for a favourable opportunity and attack us at an advantage, or protect Natal and British South Africa by a policy of firmness and consistency? The latter alternative was chosen by Her Majesty's High Commissioner; and on the 4th of January, 1879, Sir Bartle Frere placed in the hands of Lieutenant-General Lord Chelmsford, commanding in

South Africa, the farther enforcement of all demands.[5] There can be no doubt whatever that this course was the only possible one consistent with the safety of Natal and British South Africa. Cetywayo had been long preparing for war, and had most fully determined upon it, urged on by the irrepressible warlike organization and the army, which thirsted for an opportunity of exertion and could not safely be balked. Self-preservation and self-defence rendered it absolutely necessary that an army should enter Zululand.

Early in January, 1879, four columns crossed the Tugela. The line of advance described a crescent, of which one horn rested on Luneberg, or the Pongolo, and the other, or base, terminated at the lower drift of the Tugela, close to the sea. Colonel Pearson was in command of the first column, whose centre was an intrenched camp on the summit of a bluff directly overlooking the Tugela River.

It consisted of—

Regular infantry.—1500, comprising eight companies of the Buffs under Colonel Parnell, and six companies of the 99th under Colonel Welman.

Royal Engineers.—One company, with two 7-pounder guns, under Lieutenant Lloyd.

Naval Brigade.—200 blue jackets and marines, under Captain Campbell, from H.M.S. *Active* and *Tenedos*, with three Gatling guns.

Mounted infantry.—200 of Captain Barrow's.

Mounted volunteers.—200 belonging to the D'Urban Mounted

---

5. The High Commissioner writes: "Government has done its best to avoid war by every means consistent with, honour, and now feels bound to use the power with which it has been entrusted to secure the future peace and safety alike of her Majesty's dominions in South Africa, and of the Zulus and all other neighbouring tribes and people."—Memorandum of his Excellency the High Commissioner, 13th January, 1879.

With reference to the disputed Transvaal land awarded to Cetywayo, it has been argued that the territory in question should have been handed over to this savage potentate without any reference to the rights of private proprietors who had settled down and acquired domiciles. The Chief Justice of the Cape Colony, Sir J. H. De Villiers (Blue Book. July, 1879), gives a very lengthy and interesting opinion upon this subject. His Honour holds that if negotiations had been entered into between the British Government and Cetywayo for the purpose of a convention defining the mutual rights of the parties, the equitable view would have been entitled to as much weight as the legal view. The arguments used by Sir Bartle Frere are so weighty, that if they had been addressed to a potentate who is capable of understanding them, and at the same time is open to reason, they would certainly have induced him to relinquish his private rights to the land, retaining only his sovereign rights.

Rifles (Captain W. Shepstone); Alexander Mounted Rifles (Captain Arbuthnot); Victoria Mounted Rifles (Captain Sauer); Stanger Mounted Rifles (Captain Addison); the Natal Hussars (Captain Norton). To all this must be added a native contingent of 2000, under Major Graves, and two companies of the 99th, posted at Stanger and D'Urban. This was the coast column.

The second column was planted at a commanding position called Krantz Kop, inaccessible except on the Natal side. It comprised 3300 natives, with 200 European officers, supported by two rocket tubes under Lieutenant Russell, R.E., and 250 mounted natives.

The headquarters of the third column was at Helpmakaar, situated on high and open ground commanding an extensive prospect. The depôts were at Grey Town and Ladysmith. This column was exceptionally strong, and consisted of seven companies of the 1-24th, and eight of the 2-24th; six 7-pounder guns with special Kaffrarian carriages; a squadron of mounted infantry under Captain Browne; the Natal Mounted Police, 150 strong; the Natal Carbineers (Captain Shepstone); the Buffalo Border Guard (Captain Robson); the Newcastle Mounted Rifles (Captain Bradstreet); 2000 of the Native Contingent, 2nd Regiment, under Commandant Lonsdale, and 2000 natives under Colonel Glyn. General Lord Chelmsford, commander-in-chief, accompanied the column.

The fourth column had Utrecht as its base, and rested its line on the Blood River, thus covering the disputed Transvaal border. It comprised the 13th and 90th Regiments, six guns, Buller's Light Horse, and a number of natives. It consisted of about 2000 well-seasoned, reliable men, exclusive of the natives, and was under the command of Colonel Evelyn Wood, V.C.

On the 10th of January, 1879, the full period expired for the Zulu king to meet the demands of her Majesty's High Commissioner. On the 11th of January No. 3 column, under Colonel Glyn, crossed the Buffalo River into Zululand. Heavy rains had made the roads very bad, and caused the Tugela to rise so much that a barrel-raft, a pont, and a boat had to be made use of for the passage of the troops. No opposition whatever was made by the enemy. In the meantime the fourth column, under Colonel Wood, had been halted at Bemba's Kop, distant about thirty-five miles from Rorke's Drift.

On the 11th of January, Lord Chelmsford, with the bulk of the mounted men of No. 3 column, met Colonel Wood with his "irregulars" about twenty miles from Rorke's Drift, and was completely satisfied with the efficiency of the latter force, and attributed the satisfactory state of Wood's column to its commander's energy and military knowledge.[6]

On the 12th of January, Lord Chelmsford wrote:

We have had our first fight today. I ordered the whole force out this morning to reconnoitre the road along which we shall eventually have to pass. In passing by the Nkudu Hill, we noticed that some herds of cattle had been driven up close under the *krantz* where one of Sirayo's strongholds was said to be. I ordered Colonel Glyn, with four companies 1-24th, and the 1-3rd Native Contingent, to work up under the *krantz* in skirmishing order. On the approach of this force near the *krantz*, fire was opened upon them out of the caves, and the fight commenced. It lasted about half an hour, and ended in our obtaining possession of all the caves and all the cattle. Colonel Degacher, who had been sent for from camp when we found that the *krantz* was occupied by the enemy, came up towards the end of the affair with half-battalion 2-24th, and about 400 of the 2-3rd Native Contingent.

This force went forward to Sirayo's own *kraal*, which is situated under a very steep *krantz* filled with caves. The British soldiers and natives skirmished, or rather clambered, up the steep mountainside, and entered all the caves, which were found empty. I ordered Sirayo's *kraal* to be burned, but none of the other huts were touched. The Native Contingent behaved very well, and not a native touched a woman or child, or killed the wounded men.[7]

Subsequently Colonel Russell, with a small detached force, was attacked by sixty of the enemy, but his men dismounted and succeeded in killing nine or ten, among whom was one of Sirayo's sons. This action was, in fact, the storming of the stronghold of one of Cetewayo's principal chiefs, and was accompanied by the capture of 500 cattle. Lord Chelmsford says of this engagement, "I have visited two wounded Zulus who were in our hospital, and have seen that they are well looked after. Directly they are well enough I shall let them go, so

6. Despatch of the Lieutenant-General commanding-in-chief to the Secretary of State, 14th January, 1879.

7. Extract from semi-official letter to the High Commissioner, dated 12th January, 1879.

that they may tell their friends how the British make war."

Both previous to the successful and unresisted crossing of the Tugela, as well as subsequently, frequent rains had caused great discomfort to the troops, as well as immensely increased the difficulties of transport. The *impedimenta* of the large force in the field was exceedingly great, and the want of knowledge of the character of the roads, or tracks, and the capacity of oxen to do the work, resulted in many delays and difficulties. Large masses of infantry were moved into the enemy's country, whose entire dependence for supplies was placed upon heavy wagons drawn by numerous oxen. No system of carriers was established, and, with the exception of the fourth (Wood's) column, the movement of the troops was necessarily exceedingly slow.

On the march each column was exposed to be attacked at a disadvantage, so enormous was the train of wagons which had to be guarded, and the knowledge of these facts evidently enabled the Zulus to perceive the best opportunity of striking a fatal blow. At a very early stage in the war, Lord Chelmsford saw the difficulties connected with the mode of supplies adopted, as he writes on the 16th of January:

> It would be impossible to keep a long line of road passable for a
> convoy of wagons, and were we to advance far into the country
> it would be almost certain that, instead of our supplies coming
> to us, we should have to return for our supplies.

The country into which the British troops had entered was one in which the mountainsides are furrowed by deep *kloofs* or ravines, generally covered by luxuriant vegetation. The euphorbia, the cactus, the aloe, and mimosa grow in profusion, and the bush in many places forms a natural fortress, in which savages can easily lie in wait to surprise an enemy. It was in such native fastnesses that the Kafirs of the Cape Colony loved to wait—panther-like—either in war to attack the white man, or in peace to rob his flocks and herds. The Zulus, however, fortunately adopted tactics of a different character. Their plan was to attack in the open field, and, by means of braver; and overwhelming numbers, to entirely crush the enemy. It was thus that Chaka had conquered, and it was upon the same system that Cetywayo relied.

CHAPTER 4

The Battle of Isandhlwana

It is desirable for the sake of justice that the plans of Lord Chelmsford in commencing the campaign should be given in his own words. They are contained in a memorandum dated 16th January, 1879, and are as follows:—

The reports which I receive from officers commanding the several columns now operating against Cetywayo show clearly that at this season of the year a rapid advance into the heart of Zululand is absolutely impossible.

The present state of the roads in Natal will be sufficient to bring home to the mind of everyone what difficulties must stand in the way of those who are endeavouring to move forward into the enemy's country, over tracts which have never been traversed, except by a very few traders' wagons.

No. 3 column at Rorke's Drift cannot possibly move forward even eight miles, until two swamps, into which our wagons sank up to the body, have been made passable.

This work will occupy us for at least four days, and we shall find similar obstacles in front of us, in every march we are anxious to make.

Accepting the situation, therefore, it remains for me to determine what modification of the plan of campaign at first laid down will be necessary.

I consider that my original idea of driving, as far as possible, all the Zulus forward towards the north-east part of their country, is still thoroughly sound.

Without, therefore, attempting to push forward faster than our means will admit of, I propose with Nos. 1, 2, and 3 columns to thoroughly clear or subjugate the country between the Buffalo and Tugela Rivers and the Umhlatoosi River, by means of expeditions made by those columns from certain fixed positions. No. 1 column will, as already instructed, occupy Etshowe.

Instead, however, of crossing the Umhlatoosi River to Mr. Samuelson's mission station (St. Paul's), it will move a portion of its force to Entumeni, and occupy that position as well as Etshowe.

Having established itself firmly in those two positions, the main object of this column will be to clear the Inkandhla bush and forest, or to induce the chiefs and headmen of the tribes residing or specially stationed in that part of the country to tender their submission.

No. 3 column will first advance to a position near the Insandhla Hill, and from there, assisted by a portion of No. 2 column, will clear the Equideni Forest, or induce the chiefs, etc., to submit.

This work completed, the portion of No. 2 column under Lieutenant-Colonel Durnford will move towards the mission station near the Empandleni Hill, whilst No. 3 column advances to a fresh position near the Isipezi Hill, detaching, if necessary, part of its force to support No. 2 column.

These combined moves will, I hope, have the effect of removing any dangerously large body from the Natal border.

Colonel Wood, commanding No. 4 column, has been informed of these intended movements, and has been instructed to act together independently about the head waters of the White Umvoloosi River.

When Cetywayo has either surrendered or been defeated, which can only take a few more days to decide, Colonel Wood will take up a position covering Utrecht and the adjacent Transvaal border, wherever he considers his force can be most usefully employed. He will not attempt to advance towards the Inhlazatze Mountain until an advance by the other three columns across the Umhlatoosi River has become possible.

By these movements I hope to be able to clear that portion of Zululand which is situated south of the Umhlatoosi River, and behind a straight line drawn from the head waters of that river to the head waters of the White Umvoloosi River.

Should the Swazies come down to the Pongolo River, that part of Zululand which is behind a straight line drawn from the head waters of the Umvoloosi River to the junction of the Bevan and Pongolo Rivers, will also, no doubt, be abandoned, and possibly as far as the Lebombo Mountains.

I trust that this plan of campaign will meet with the approval of the High Commissioner.

From a military point of view I am convinced that it is the only practicable one at this time of year, and if successfully carried out, is capable of producing very satisfactory results.

I am equally confident that, politically, it will also have good results,

We shall occupy a large extent of Zululand, and shall threaten the portion which remains to the king. We shall completely cover the Natal border, and shall to a considerable extent do the same for the Transvaal. We expect Cetywayo to keep his army mobilized, and it is clear his troops will have difficulty in finding sufficient supplies.

On the 20th of January, 1879, the camp of the third column was at the Isandhlwana Mountain. This force was under the command of Colonel Glyn, C.B., and the general commanding had accompanied it from the Tugela River. On the date just quoted, orders were given to Commandant Lonsdale and Major Dartnell to go out the following morning, and make a forward movement with a force composed of Native Contingent, Police, and Volunteers.

On the next day (21st January), Major Dartnell sent in word that the enemy was near him in considerable force. Upon this Lord Chelmsford ordered the 2nd Battalion, 24th Regiment, the mounted infantry, and four guns, to be under arms at once, and this force left so soon as there was light enough to see the road. Before Lord Chelmsford left, he sent the following order to Lieutenant-Colonel Durnford, commanding No. 2 column:—

Move up to Isandhlwana camp at once with all your mounted men and rocket battery. Take command of it. I am accompanying Colonel Glyn, who is moving off at once to attack Matyana and a Zulu force said to be twelve or fourteen miles off, and at present watched by Natal Police, Volunteers, and Natal Native Contingent. Colonel Glyn takes with him 2-24th Regiment, four guns R.A., and Mounted Infantry."[6]

Major Clery, senior staff officer to the third column, says—

6. Lieutenant-Colonel Crealock—Statement to Court-Martial.

"Before leaving the camp I sent written instructions to Colonel Pulleine, 24th Regiment, to the following effect:—'You will be in command of the camp during the absence of Colonel Glyn. Draw in' (I speak from memory) 'your camp, or your line of defence,'—I am not certain which—'while the force is out. Also draw in the line of your infantry outposts accordingly; but keep your cavalry *vedettes* still far advanced.' I went to Colonel Pulleine's tent just before leaving camp, to ascertain that he had got those instructions, and I again repeated them verbally to him." [7]

Captain Alan Gardiner, of the 14th Hussars, states that he left the camp with Lord Chelmsford on the 22nd of January, and was sent back into camp with an order from the general, between 10 and 11 a.m. that day. Colonel Pulleine was informed that the camp of the force out was to be struck, and sent on immediately; "also rations and forage for about seven days." This order came too late. At the moment of its receipt Colonel Durnford was falling back and begging Colonel Pulleine to send him reinforcements, and the enemy began to appear in large numbers.

In order to make the proceedings of this fatal day more easily understood, it is now necessary to advert to the proceedings of the Zulu army. This was 20,000 strong, and consisted of the Undi corps, the Nokenke and Umcityo regiments, and the Nkobamakosi and Inbonambi regiments. These comprised the flower of Cetywayo's troops. During the night of the 21st of January they were ordered to move in small detached bodies to a position about a mile and a half to the east of the camp at Isandhlwana, on a stony table-land, only about 1000 yards distant from the spot visited by Lord Chelmsford and Colonel Glyn on the afternoon of the 21st of January.

No fires were lighted, and the stillness of death was preserved. The centre was occupied by the Undi corps, the right wing by the Nokenke and Umcityu, and the left by the Inbonambi and the Nkobamakosi regiments. The king's orders comprised a simple command to drive the third column back into Natal. But there was no intention whatever of making an attack upon the 22nd of January. The state of the moon was unfavourable, the usual medicine sprinkling had not taken place, nor had the war-song been chanted. What superstition forbade was, however, conceded to expediency. When the divi-

---

7. Major Clery, chief of the staff, third column—Evidence before Court-Martial.

sion of the British forces was noticed, and their gross ignorance and carelessness observed, the Zulu leaders felt like Cromwell, when he exclaimed, with reference to the Scottish army, "*The Lord has delivered them into our hands.*"

On the morning of the 22nd of January, the mounted Basutos sent out under the command of Colonel Durnford fired upon the Umcityu regiment. This was too favourable an opportunity to be neglected. Here was a portion only of the third column, with an unfortified camp, whose defenders were scattering themselves over a large space, utterly ignorant and careless of the fact that the overwhelming and concentrated Zulu force was close beside them. The charge of the Umcityu regiment was immediately and vigorously followed by that of the Nokenke, Inbonambi, and Nkobamikosi regiments, the Undi corps holding its ground.

Up to this time in the day there had been no fighting. Early in the morning, not long after the departure of the general, a body of the Native Contingent had been sent out to scout, and either did not see or pretended not to see any enemy. About 9 a.m. Colonel Durnford, R.E., arrived with 250 mounted men and 250 native infantry, who were at once divided into three bodies and scattered to the left east, the left front, and the rear. So far from a plan of concentration being adopted, the very opposite course was pursued. It was the force sent to the left east that was attacked by the Zulu army.

No further concealment was now necessary, and messengers arrived informing Colonel Durnford that an enormous force was advancing. A consultation then took place between that officer and Colonel Pulleine, when some difference of opinion seemed to prevail. A company of the 1st Battalion, 24th Regiment, was then immediately moved up to a distance of about a mile and a half from the camp, where, at a neck of the Isandhlwana Hill, an attempt was made to cheek the advance of the Zulu army. For a very short time only this manoeuvre was successful.

The Zulu army now advanced in a steady, quiet, and determined manner. The Umcityu regiment formed the right centre, and was engaged with one company of the 1st Battalion, 24th Regiment, and about 200 of Colonel Durnford's natives; the left centre was composed of the Nokenke regiment, which was shelled by the two guns as it advanced. Next on the left, came the Imbonambi regiment, with the Nkobamakosi regiment outside of it, both making a turning movement and threatening the front of the camp, while driving before

43

them a body of Colonel Durnford's mounted men, supported by a patrol of volunteers.[8]

The Undi corps, on seeing that the other four regiments had commenced the attack, concealed themselves on the north side of the Isandhlwana Mountain, and so turned as to arrive at the western front where the wagon road crosses the neck. On the left front of the camp our infantry behaved with extreme gallantry, and succeeded in thrice repulsing the Nkobamakosi regiment; but the Inbonambi regiment coming up as a reinforcement, enabled the Zulus to push forward along the south front of the camp and accomplish their turning movement. The guns were moved to the right of the Native Contingent, and troops lined the *nullah* below; three companies of the 1-24th remained on the left of the camp, supported by Durnford's mounted Basutos, who had been driven back. The single company of the 124-th, which had been thrown out a mile and a half from the camp, was retiring, fighting to the best of their ability, and, of course, was cut off to a man.

The Zulu army was fast surrounding the camp. They had been held only partially in check by our fire, and their own was remarkably ineffective. Their overwhelming numbers and their extremely advantageous position filled them with redoubled courage. In place of advancing steadily and in silence, they now began to double and to shout exultantly to each other. the Native Contingent and camp-followers fled in all directions, seized by panic; the Undi corps showed itself on the right rear of the camp, cutting off retreat to Rorke's Drift, and a hand-to-hand combat against overwhelming odds was imminent.

Like the sea breaking against land, the Zulu host came on invincibly, with overwhelming power and strength. Then took place one of the most awful tragedies ever recorded in the page of history. With short stabbing *assegais*, on rushed the naked savages, accompanying the death groans of their victims with yells and shouts of triumph. No mercy was either expected or granted. Hundreds of men, overpowered by brute force, fell at their posts, and their fate was rendered more pitiable, as well as more blameable, by a failure in the supply of ammunition.

From first to last, nothing could have been worse managed than the defence of our camp at Isandhlwana. Profound ignorance and rashness caused the dispersion of a force which, if formed in hollow square—

8. See Statement by *Natives, and Statement by W. Drummond, Headquarters Staff*.—Blue Books.

or better still, *laagered* in accordance with the Dutch custom—would have defied the enemy, at least until such time as the general, with the rest of the third column, could have arrived. The lamentable spectacle was seen at Isandhlwana of brave soldiers sacrificed through the most glaring incompetency and folly.

For the British infantry there was no opportunity of escape—death at their post on the field of battle was inevitable; but for the mounted men a chance occurred in consequence of the Nkobamakosi regiment neglecting to make a junction with the Undi. This was taken advantage of by a crowd of fugitives. In the flight many were killed before the Buffalo River was reached, and many were drowned and shot when trying to cross it. The Zulus, however, had themselves suffered severely. The Umcityu lost heavily from the fire of the single company of the 24th Regiment which was sent out from camp never to return, the Nkobamakosi fell in heaps, and the hill down which the Nokenke came was covered with slain.

As regards the British troops, our loss comprised 62 men of the N Battery, 5th Brigade, Royal Artillery; 7 of the Royal Engineers, including Colonel Durnford; 405 of the 1st Battalion, 24th Regiment, including Lieutenant-Colonel Pulleine, Captains Degacher, Mostyn, Wardell, and Younghusband (Lieutenant and Adjutant Melvill was killed on the western side of the Buffalo River, when most gallantly defending the colours of his regiment, which were afterwards found wrapped round his body); 165 men of the 2nd Battalion, 24th Regiment; Surgeon-Major Shepherd, Army Medical Department; 12 Mounted Infantry; 26 Natal Mounted Police; 22 Natal Carbineers; 7 Newcastle Mounted Rifles, and 3 Buffalo Borderguard; 37 of the 1st Battalion, 3rd Regiment, Natal Native Contingent; 37 of the 2nd Battalion, 3rd Regiment, Natal Native Contingent. Among the Carbineers and other volunteer corps were the sons of many of the leading inhabitants of Natal, and in the Police also were many relatives of colonists.

The official lists comprising white men killed, publish more than 770 names; but there is no doubt that, including the loyal natives, quite 1000 of our men must have been slain. All the baggage, guns, and ammunition became the property of the enemy, and in the incredibly short space of one hour from the beginning of the general attack, one of the most signal victories possible had been gained by the Zulu army. The number of white men who escaped across the Buffalo River was about forty, in addition to natives on horseback and foot. Of the former, about twenty-five or thirty arrived at Helpmakaar between 5 and 6 p.m. The Undi corps, believing that the camp had been plundered by the other portions of their army, thought it desirable to advance quickly on Rorke's Drift to secure the booty there, and hurried off for this destination, little dreaming of the possibility of any resistance.

While these occurrences had been taking place, Lord Chelmsford, with Colonel Glyn and a large portion of the third column, were absent in advance. On the 20th of January, the general had made a reconnoissance as far as a place called Matyana's stronghold—a deep valley, full of caves. Not having time to examine this place thoroughly, two separate parties were ordered out to bring back a full description of it. One of these, under Major Dartnell, reported that he found the enemy in force, and would be able to attack if three companies of infantry were sent to him. This was not acceded to. At 2.30 a.m. on the 22nd of January, Colonel Glyn was ordered to move to Dartnell's assistance with six companies 2-24th, four guns, and the mounted infantry. Colonel Durnford was at the same time ordered up to strengthen the Isandhlwana camp. The general followed Colonel Glyn's reinforcements, and reached Major Dartnell at 6.30 a.m. The enemy shortly showed at a distance, but retreated when a general advance was made. All this was, no doubt, part of the Zulu plan of amusing this portion of our forces, and keeping them from the Isandhlwana camp.

The only actual engagement that took place was at the extreme right, where 500 Zulus were cut off, of whom 30 were killed. At 9 a.m. a short note was received from Lieutenant-Colonel Pulleine, stating that firing had been heard, but giving no further particulars. Lieutenant Milne, A.D.C., was sent by the general to the top of a high hill from which the camp could be seen, and he remained there for at least an hour, with a very powerful telescope, but could detect nothing unusual in that direction. A site for a new camp was then fixed upon, and the troops were ordered to bivouac there that night. The general then started to return to camp with the mounted infantry under Colonel Russell. When within six miles from Isandhlwana, Lord Chelmsford found the 1st Battalion, Native Contingent, halted, and shortly after Commandant Lonsdale rode up to report that he had ridden into camp, and found it in possession of the Zulus.

Intimation had been received so far back as between 9.30 and 10 a.m.[9] that there was a force of the enemy in the close neighbourhood

9. See Statement of Lieutenant-Colonel Crealock, Acting Military Secretary.

of the camp. Major Clery at this time received a half sheet of foolscap from Lieutenant-Colonel Pulleine, giving him that information, and as the force was only twelve miles from camp, an immediate rapid advance would have saved the day. The exact words of this letter are not given in the evidence, and are clearly of the utmost consequence.

It was after this, however, that Lieutenant Milne, A.D.C., descended the hill, with the report that he noticed nothing except the cattle being driven into camp. This fact, however, was of great consequence, taken in connection with the pressing nature of the despatch from Colonel Pulleine. Notwithstanding all this, nothing was suspected until the dreadful news came like a thunder-clap, that the camp had been taken and its defenders killed. So soon as the general heard the awful news, he sent back Major Gossett, A.D.C, to order Colonel Glyn to advance with all his force. He was six miles off, and it was then 4 p.m.

The advance party, with the general, continued to go forward, until they were within two miles from the camp, when they halted. Colonel Russell went to the front to reconnoitre, and returned about 5.45 with a report that "all was as bad as could be." The Zulus held the camp. At 6 p.m. Colonel Glyn came up with his troops, which, having been formed into fighting order, were addressed by the general. No sign of wavering was perceptible. They advanced with steady courage, determined to attack and go through any enemy. Guns in the centre; three companies 2-24th on each flank in fours; Native Contingent; mounted infantry on extreme right. Natal Mounted Volunteers on the extreme left; Mounted Police in reserve;—in this order the force went forward with great speed.

The artillery shelled the crest of the narrow neck over which the line of retreat lay, and positions were seized without opposition. The curtain of night had fallen over the dreadful scene of carnage, and the entire force, tired and dispirited, lay down amidst the *débris* of the plundered camp and the corpses of men, horses, and oxen. The weariness and sorrow of these hours of darkness will never be forgotten. The troops fully expected to be attacked in front and rear; but fortunately the Zulus knew better how to gain than how to improve a victory, and although there were several alarms, not a shot was fired, and Lord Chelmsford, with the remnant of his forces, was able at dawn of day to hurry on to the relief of Rorke's Drift.

On the 22nd of January, Lieutenant Chard, E.E., was left in command at Rorke's Drift by Major Spalding, who went to Helpmakaar to hurry on the company of the 24th Regiment ordered to protect the ponts. About 3.15 p.m. of that day, two men came riding furiously from Zululand, and shouted to be taken across the river. These were Lieutenant Adendorff, of Lonsdale's regiment, and a carbineer. The former remained to assist in the defence; the latter galloped off to take the intelligence to Helpmakaar.

The news was of the frightful disaster at Isandhlwana—that the Zulus were advancing on the colony in force, and that Rorke's Drift must, therefore, be held at all cost. Lieutenant Bromhead, who commanded the company of the 24th Regiment at the camp near the commissariat stores, had just then received a note from the third column, and sent for Lieutenant Chard. Preparations for defence were made with the utmost vigour. Separate buildings were connected by walls of *mealie*-bags and two wagons; the store building and hospital were loopholed and barricaded. All available materials were made use of, and the brave little garrison determined to repulse the enemy or die behind their frail entrenchments.

At the river the ferryman, Daniells, and Sergeant Milne, 3rd Buffs, offered to moor the pont in the middle of the stream, and with a few men fight from its deck; but this offer was declined, and the brave fellows who made it were enrolled among the garrison.

The sound of firing was heard at 4.20 p.m. Previously, an officer of Durnford's had been requested to send outposts in the direction of the enemy, and to check their advances as much as possible. His men, however, would not obey orders, and rode off, 100 in number, to Helpmakaar. About the same time, Captain Stephenson, with his detachment of Natal Native Contingent, left the little garrison. The line of defence was at once seen to be too extended for the small number of men that were left, and a new entrenchment of biscuit-boxes had at once to be commenced.

The wall had only been built two boxes high, when, at 4.30 p.m., 600 Zulus were seen advancing at a run against the south wall. They were met by a well-sustained fire, but, notwithstanding their heavy loss, continued to advance within fifty yards. Here they encountered the additional cross-fire from the store and were checked. Unfortunately, however, some were able to take advantage of the shelter afforded by the cook-house ovens, etc. By far the larger number never stopped, but moved to the left, round the hospital, and made a rush at the north-west wall of *mealie*-bags. A desperate bayonet struggle took place here, which resulted in the repulse of the enemy with heavy loss.

The bush in the immediate neighbourhood, which had not been cut down, enabled the Zulus to advance under cover close to the wall. A number of desperate assaults were made, all of which were most splendidly met and repulsed by the bayonet.

A very harassing fire was encountered from the rocks, which caused severe loss, and about 6 p.m. obliged a retreat behind the entrenchment of the biscuit-boxes. While all this was going on, the Zulus had been attempting to force the hospital, and shortly afterwards set fire to its roof. The garrison there most gallantly defended the building from floor to floor, bringing out all the sick that could be moved. Four privates of the 24th Regiment (Williams, Hook, R. Jones, and W. Jones) were the last men to leave, holding the doorway with the bayonet, their own ammunition being exhausted.

Mealie-bags were then converted into a sort of redoubt, which gave a second line of fire all round. While this was being done, the hospital was in flames, and the enemy continued to make desperate attempts to fire the roof of the stores. Shortly before darkness came on, the gallant little force was completely surrounded, and, after repulsing several attacks, felt compelled to retire to the centre of their entrenchments, the vigour of the siege continued until after midnight, and then it lapsed into a desultory fire, which was kept up all night.

About 4 a.m. on the 23rd of January, the firing ceased, and at daybreak the enemy was out of sight over the hill to the south-west. The number of the defending force was exactly 104,[10] and that of the Zulus who attacked about 3000. No fewer than 350 of the enemy were killed. Thus was the colony of Natal saved by the undaunted resolution of a little band of heroes whose conduct rivals that of the men of Thermopylæ.

At about 7 a.m. a large body of the enemy were seen advancing. No reinforcements had arrived from Helpmakaar, although they had been specially sent for, and the ammunition was almost expended. At about 8 a.m. the third column providentially appeared in sight, and Lord Chelmsford and staff soon afterwards galloped up to Rorke's Drift and warmly congratulated its gallant defenders. They had by their undaunted bravery and firm attitude before an overwhelming force of the enemy done much to neutralize the effect of the disaster at Isandhlwana, and Lord Chelmsford himself officially reports, "no doubt saved Natal from a serious invasion." He adds, "The cool, de-

---

10. This excludes the sick, who were thirty-five in number.

termined courage displayed by the gallant garrison is beyond all praise, and will, I feel sure, receive ample recognition."

The disaster at Isandhlwana, looked at correctly, confirms most strongly the arguments advanced by the High Commissioner in favour of the war. It became perfectly evident that the Zulu king had an army at his command which could, almost any day, unexpectedly invade Natal; and, owing to the great extent of frontier and character of the natives within the colony, they might have devastated the country without the possibility of being adequately cheeked. To use the words of Sir Bartle Frere, it would have been vain—almost criminal—to ignore the fact that there had grown up by our sufferance alongside Natal a very powerful military organization, directed by an irresponsible, bloodthirsty, and treacherous despot. This extraordinary power simply made the existence of a peaceful English community so precarious as to prevent its safe continuance in any other form than that of an armed camp.

So soon as the news of Isandhlwana reached the colony, a terrible panic was the result. The inhabitants fled to the towns, *laagers* were formed in every direction, while in D'Urban and Pietermaritzburg entrenchments and fortifications were at once erected. The heroic defence of Rorke'a Drift and the providential flooding of the Tugela river were the means of saving the colony. Flushed with victory, nothing would have been able to withstand the Zulu armies, if they had crossed the boundary and, in their well-organized form, entered Natal.

As a result of the Isandhlwana disaster, the native allies could no longer be trusted, and melted away by means of desertion. Lord Chelmsford was obliged to report that large British reinforcements were absolutely required if the operations against the Zulus were to be carried to a successful issue. Three British infantry regiments, two cavalry regiments, and one company of Royal Engineers, as well as 100 artillerymen, were asked for. When the request reached England, it was immediately granted, but a fearful period of suspense and anxiety intervened. It is difficult to portray in words the feelings of the white inhabitants of Natal, who every moment expected to hear that a savage, ruthless foe was in full march for the purpose of utterly exterminating the hated white race.

Sixty miles only intervened between D'Urban and the Tugela River; Pietermaritzburg was still more exposed. Numbers of people fled to the seaboard, and thence to the neighbouring colony; while, behind *laagers* and hastily constructed fortifications, the people waited in expectant terror for every item of news from the theatre of war. In the Cape Colony, the most vigorous measures were adopted by its Government.

Two hundred volunteers from Cape Town, and 100 from Port Elizabeth, proceeded immediately to King William's Town and relieved the 88th Regiment, ordered to Natal; 900 mounted yeomanry were called out to occupy certain positions on the border, in conjunction with 600 Cape Mounted Riflemen.

Two thousand Europeans were thus placed under arms, 1700 of whom were mounted men. This was really necessary in order to keep down possible insurrections of Pondos, Basutos, and Griquas. All the black races throughout Southern Africa had to be feared, as they only waited an opportunity to make common cause against the Europeans. Already in detail had the Gealekas and the Gaikas been thoroughly defeated, but the Basutos and Pondos had hitherto hung back. The Zulu war was watched by them with lively feelings of interest, and their sympathies were, of course, enlisted on the side of Cetywayo.

Her Majesty the Queen, with the utmost sympathy and promptness, caused the Secretary of State to telegraph, on the 18th of February, her sorrow at the loss of so many brave officers and men of the regular and colonial forces, and her full confidence that Lord Chelmsford would be able to meet the difficulties in which he was placed. The message ended with the words, "Full reinforcements of all arms will be sent with the utmost despatch."

The Imperial Ministry was fiercely attacked in England for having entered upon the Zulu war, and succumbed to the pressure of public opinion so far as to blame Sir Bartle Frere for taking, without their full knowledge and sanction, a course almost certain to result in war, which every effort; should have been used to avoid. The High Commissioner, under his commission, was not only empowered, but really authorized and obliged, to enter upon this war. His Excellency knew that it was necessary to open the campaign at once in Zululand; and the mild, modified rebuke of the Conservative Ministry was evidently wrong from them more by the exigencies of party than by the actual circumstances.

A disaster always evokes a cry for victims, and the British populace were loud in the usual *væ victus* clamour. Sir Bartle Frere, however, stood firm, strong in the confidence of eventually obtaining justice; while the Ministry at home were sufficiently powerful and sufficiently noble to refuse to sacrifice Lord Chelmsford to the ferocious outcry that was raised against him.

CHAPTER 5

Zulu Raids

We have now to advert to the proceedings of No. 1 column, comprising 1200 British troops, under the command of Lieutenant-Colonel Pearson. Having crossed the Tugela River, an advance was commenced towards Ekowe on the 18th of January. No fewer than 130 wagons, as well as a number of other vehicles, accompanied this column, whose order of march was as follows:—

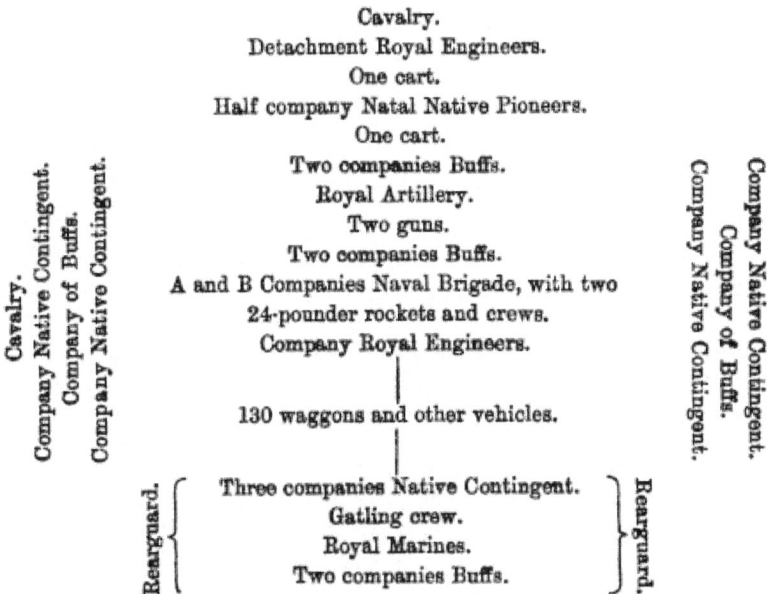

Cavalry.
Detachment Royal Engineers.
One cart.
Half company Natal Native Pioneers.
One cart.
Two companies Buffs.
Royal Artillery.
Two guns.
Two companies Buffs.
A and B Companies Naval Brigade, with two
24-pounder rockets and crews.
Company Royal Engineers.

130 waggons and other vehicles.

Three companies Native Contingent.
Gatling crew.
Royal Marines.
Two companies Buffs.

Left side (read bottom to top): Cavalry. Company Native Contingent. Company of Buffs. Company Native Contingent.

Right side: Company Native Contingent. Company of Buffs. Company Native Contingent.

Rearguard. (left and right)

The difficulties of transport were considerable, and the immense train of wagons not only delayed progress, but made an attack, when the troops were in motion, more difficult to resist. Nothing of consequence occurred on the march, excepting the destruction of a large military *kraal*. The enemy, however, hovered about the column, and only waited for a favourable opportunity.

At last, on the 22nd of January, the day of Isandhlwana, the march was commenced at 5 a.m. After passing five miles along a fertile valley, the path turned suddenly to the left, and the ascent of the high land on which Ekowe is situated commenced. The head of the column reached the turning, and was preparing to halt for breakfast, when it was suddenly attacked along the entire right flank and on both fronts. The Zulus had been lying in ambush. Rushing from bush to bush, and firing with great rapidity, they advanced in extended order so as to come within a distance of 160 yards. Their advance was checked by the heavy fire from two 7-pounders, Royal Artillery, and two 24-pounder Naval Brigade rockets, placed on a knoll at the foot of the pass commanding the valley from which the flank attack proceeded. Two companies of the Buffs, as well as A and B companies of the Naval Brigade, assisted in holding this position, and poured in a steady fire.

While these proceedings were going on under the personal direction of Colonel Pearson, the wagons continued to park, and as soon as the length of the column had sufficiently decreased, two companies of the Buffs, which had been guarding the wagons, were directed to clear the enemy out of the bush. Led by Captains Harrison and Wild, they got into skirmishing order, and in good style drove the Zulus back into the open plain, where they were effectually swept by rockets, shells, and musketry. The main body of the mounted infantry, under Major Barrow and Captain Wynne, were now able to move forward. An attempt to outflank on the part of the enemy was defeated by the Naval Brigade and a part of the Native Contingent. Shortly afterwards, a brilliant and successful attack was made upon heights where a considerable body of Zulus were posted. The Zulus then fled in all directions, and a complete victory was gained.

The plan of fighting by the Zulus was in accordance with their usual well-organized scheme. The formation of their attack is in the figure of a beast, with horns, chest, and loins. They usually make a feint with one horn, whilst the other, concealed by long grass or bush, sweeps round for the purpose of encompassing its enemy. The chest

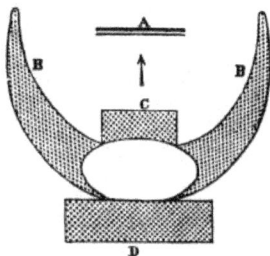

A. The enemy.	C. Chest of Zulu army.
BB. Horns of Zulu army.	D. Loins of Zulu army.

then advances, and endeavours by its vast power to crush opposition. The loins are kept at a distance and only join in pursuit.

The action of Inyezani lasted exactly one hour and a half, commencing at 8 a.m. and the last shot being fired at 9.30 a.m. The British loss was 12 killed and 16 wounded, while of the Zulus 300 were slain. It is conjectured that the attacking force comprised nearly 5000 men.

After the battle was over the column calmly resumed the even tenor of its way, and at night bivouacked on a high ridge distant only three miles from the battlefield. The road led up a winding and steep ascent, and on the 23rd of January, after marching six miles further, Ekowe was reached. The intention was to leave surplus stores here, with a small garrison, and push on to Cetywayo's kraal at Ulundi. But these plans had to be completely changed. On the 29th of January, about noon, a messenger galloped in from Lord Chelmsford with the news of the fearful disaster at Isandhlawana, and that the entire Zulu army might be expected to attack them. Colonel Pearson had to decide either, to hold the fort, or to march back, at once and quickly, to the Tugela River. A council of war was assembled, and, by a small majority, it was resolved to maintain their position at all costs. The result proved that this was a wise determination.

In order to husband resources, all the cavalry, with the two battalions of Native Contingent, were sent back, and by this means the garrison lost all means of obtaining information of the enemy's movements. The Victoria, Stanger, and D'Urban Mounted Rifles, as well as the Natal Hussars, and two battalions of the Natal Native Contingent, rode away at 2 p.m. of the day on which the order was given, and at midnight arrived safely on the banks of the Tugela, not having seen a Zulu on the way. Colonel Ely, *en route* with supplies, was directed to hasten on to Ekowe, and, in order to do so more effectually, abandoned eight wagons, with their contents of flour, biscuit, limejuice, sugar, etc.

On the 30th of January, all the troops came inside the embryo fort; tents were no longer allowed, and officers and men were obliged to huddle together under wagons. The garrison consisted of 1889 whites and 856 blacks, of whom 47 whites and 290 blacks were non-combatants. The armament comprised 1200 Martini rifles, with 330 rounds per rifle; 1 Gatling, with 127,000 rounds; 2 rocket tubes, with 83 rockets; and 2 7-pounders, with 500 rounds. The garrison had 3000 oxen, but were obliged to drive away a large number, and soon learned, by the loss of 90 slaughter oxen from the ditch of the parapet, that large numbers of Zulus were close at hand. The fort soon attained a respectable appearance. It was oblong in shape—east and west sides, 300 yards each; north side, 120 yards; south, 180 yards. Wagons were placed round the inside of the parapet, a few yards distant.

The church was converted into a hospital, the schoolroom and parsonage into storerooms, and all other buildings were demolished. All hands were up at *réveille*, and engaged all day in making the fort, and, when that was completed, in making roads. At 8 p.m. the "last post" sounded, and then all gave themselves to sleep, often broken by the alarm of the church bell, when the parapets were manned at once. A few irregular horse had been enrolled, who did outpost duty during the day. At this time an army of 20,000 Zulus was lying in wait between Ekowe and the Tugela.

Lord Chelmsford desired Colonel Pearson to reduce his garrison, and to establish a portion of it at the Tugela forts; but this was clearly impossible, and it is very surprising that such an order could ever have been issued. On the 6th of February, Colonel Pearson wrote, suggesting that twenty wagons, with a convoy, should be sent. In reply, the general sent word that there would not be a force at Lower Tugela for six weeks sufficient to insure a convoy to Ekowe, but wished the garrison there reduced and a flying column formed. This was quite out of the question, and, of course, was not attempted.

On the 10th of February the fort was completed, with ditches seven feet deep and twelve feet wide, flanked by *caponnières* or by the parapet itself; wire entanglements on the glacis, and stakes in the ditch. The two 7-pounders were at the south-east and south-west angles, the rocket battery at the north-west, and the Gatling on the east face of the parapet.

The stench, at night particularly, was absolutely sickening, although every effort was made to keep the camp clean. Rations soon had to be reduced. A bottle of pickles fetched 25s.; sardines, 12s.; tin of milk, 23s.; a ham, £7 10s. There was always, however, a sufficient quantity of food of a coarse description, and the only famine that the garrison really suffered from was a dearth of news. Intelligence of how the war was going on, and of the outside world, was greedily and earnestly thirsted for. Convoys were always looked for and never arrived. No attack was ever made upon the fort by the wily Zulus, although they lay in wait for any opportunity.

The defence of Rorke's Drift had not only saved Natal from destruction, but Ekowe from attack. Affairs dragged on in a dull, monotonous manner all through February until the beginning of March. From a slight elevation near the camp the Lower Tugela could be seen, and H.M.S. *Active* cruising on the coast. Many a time were eyes stretched over the thirty-five miles of country intervening between Ekowe and Natal for some sign of relief and of succour.

An officer in Ekowe says, "The troops inside consisted of three companies of the 99th Regiment, five companies of the 2-3rd Buffs, one company Royal Engineers, one company of the Pioneers, the Naval Brigade, a body of artillery, and nineteen of the Native Contingent, amongst them being several non-commissioned officers, whom we found exceedingly useful, two of them being at once selected as butchers, whilst two others were 'promoted' to the rank of 'bakers to the troops.' Others attended to the sanitary arrangements of the garrison, and altogether they were found to be also exceedingly useful. As a portion of the column the company of pioneers under the command of Captain Beddoes did a great deal of very important work. This company was composed of ninety-eight natives, one captain, and three lieutenants, and their proceedings in connection with the making of the new road were watched with much interest. They worked with the Naval Brigade, about three companies of soldiers, and several men of the Royal Artillery.

This road was found useless in consequence of the numerous swampy places at the foot of each of the numerous hills which occurred along the route. Very thick bush had to be cut through, and at first but slow progress was made. The road, as is generally known, took a direction towards the Inyezane. Whilst out on one occasion, the road party saw a torpedo explosion, which took place about three miles from where the party was working. It had been accidentally fired by Kafirs, who were unaware of the dangers connected with the implement, and it is believed that several of them were killed. The road was altogether a bad one. The relief column used it on their way up, but only the pioneers and the mounted men went by that route on the way back. In fact, it would have been useless to have attempted to use it for the passage of wagons.

Whenever the road party went out they were fired on by Kafirs, but of course shots were returned, and many a Zulu warrior was knocked over whilst the work was being proceeded with. Everything in camp was conducted in a most orderly manner. We were roused at half-past five, sharp, and at eight o'clock, sharp, lights were out. For one month we existed very comfortably on full rations, but at the end of that time we were put on short rations, made up as follow:—One pound and a quarter of trek oxen beef, six ounces of meal, one ounce and a quarter of sugar, third of an ounce of coffee, one-sixth of an ounce of tea, one-ninth of an ounce of pepper, and a quarter of an ounce of salt. Life of course was very monotonous. The bands of the two regiments played on alternate afternoons, and every morning they were to be heard practising outside the entrenchment.

The most pleasant part of the day was just after six o'clock, when we used to be enlivened in the cool of the evening by the fife and drum band, playing the 'retreat.' The water with which we were supplied was indeed excellent, and the bathing places, I need not say, were very extensively patronized. The grazing was not nearly sufficient for the cattle, and from the first they must have suffered very much from want of nourishment. You will have heard of the fate of the 1100 head of oxen and the span of donkeys which we sent away from the camp in expectation of their reaching the Lower Tugela. They left us in charge of nineteen Kafirs; but at the Inyezane they were attacked by a large body of Kafirs.

The natives in charge of the cattle decamped and reached the fort in safety, and the enemy got possession of the whole of the cattle, which they drove off. The donkeys were all killed, with the exception of one, and this sagacious animal surprised everybody in camp by returning soon after the Kafirs had come back."

Shortly after the disaster at Isandhlwana, the main body of the Zulu army went up to the king to be doctored with charms taken from the mutilated bodies of the killed of the English army. The intended movements of Cetywayo were described as follows:—"When the doctoring is done, the king will order a still stronger force than that of 22nd January; perhaps 20,000 or 30,000 to attack in one mass

Colonel Glynn's column, and if they succeed, then attack Colonel Wood's column; but if they do not succeed in doing this, he will try to check and harass the English columns in Zululand by manoeuvring a sufficient number of soldiers around them, and simultaneously make strong impetuous raids into the colony, as he has prohibited his people making raids in small numbers; he has furthermore plainly and repeatedly expressed himself to the effect that if he is to lose his life and kingdom, he 'will first make such havoc in Natal that it forever shall be remembered.'

The truth is that something little short of a universal panic prevailed, which only by degrees subsided as time passed on without any invasion, and leisure was allowed for reflection. It does not seem to have been remembered that in every direction except one, and by all the columns except that of Colonel Glyn, the Zulus were defeated. Isandhlwana was a purely exceptional case, entirely attributable to blundering of the most gross and evident character. The defence of Rorke's Drift and the battle of Ineyezani were most significant. At the former a handful of infantry defended themselves successfully behind *mealie*-bags and biscuit-boxes against three times their number; at the latter, an overwhelming force was easily defeated in the field by the simple strategy of common sense.

No. 4 column, under Colonel Wood, operated in the north and acted as a means of defence to Utrecht and the Transvaal. It was assisted from the first by a number of irregulars and volunteers. Successful forays were made on various occasions, but it would be tedious to do more than refer to these, although the greatest gallantry and skill were exhibited. Colonel Wood most deservedly increased his reputation as a brilliant and successful leader. A fort was established at Kambula Hill, entrenched in such a manner as to defy the attacks of a savage enemy.

February was a month of suspense. Cetywayo had an opportunity of which he did not avail himself, but was contented with reorganizing and reanointing his armies. Colonel Pearson remained at Ekowe; forts were placed on the Tugela River; mounted forces were distributed along the border from Fort Pearson to Thring's Post. There was, in addition, a border guard of white officers and natives, about 1500 strong. "Stanger"—fifteen miles on the Natal side—as well as D'Urban, Maritzburg, and every town of the least consequence, was fortified, and then volunteer and citizen soldiers prepared themselves for any emergency.

The High Commissioner, Sir Bartle Frere, who had proceeded to Natal on the outbreak of hostilities, still remained at Pietermaritzburg, and was there in the best possible position for giving that advice and assistance so necessary in the serious emergencies in which a British colony and a British general were placed. Unfortunately, many of the people of Dutch extraction in the Transvaal seemed to take the opportunity for loudly protesting against the annexation of that territory, to the Crown, then recently effected by Sir Theophilus Shepstone.

A people's committee was appointed, and a firm determination expressed to regain that republican liberty of which they believed they had been unjustly deprived. One of the most satisfactory events of this month was the evident desire of the king's brother, Oham, to be regarded as our friend. His country lay in the north-west of Zululand, and at an interview held with Colonel Wood, conditions of surrender were arranged. Early in March he came in with more than 600 people.

Under the orders and with the connivance of Cetywayo, the chiefs Umbellini and Manyanyoba perpetrated the most horrid cruelties. Atrocious outrages had been committed long previously, but the Transvaal republican authorities had not apparently considered it expedient to report them fully. The little town of Luneberg was undoubtedly saved by a company of troops sent there by Colonel Wood. This officer had it in his power, when passing through Manyanyoba's country, to crush him and his warriors, but accepted in good faith the statement of that chief, professing a desire to come under the British Government.

In spite of this, on the 10th of February, a Zulu war party, led by Umbellini, crossed the Pongolo, and was joined on the north by a strong force of Manyanyoba's people, led by Manyanyoba himself.[11] The combined force consisted of 1500 men. At half-past 3 a.m. of the 11th February, they reached the mission station of the Rev. Mr. Wagner, only four miles from Luneberg, and then commenced a scene of most atrocious murder. Men, women, and children were massacred. The houses of the Christian natives were given to the flames, and no fewer than seven children were burnt alive.

From Wagner's they went to Nomapela's Kraal, where they killed two men, eleven women, and fifteen children. Thence they proceeded to Luhlanya's *kraal*, where they murdered one man, two women, and

---

11. See report from Colonel Schermbrucker to Colonel Evelyn Wood.—Parliamentary Blue Book.

two children. But it is unnecessary to prolong the narrative; suffice it to say that they went through the country with fire and sword, sparing neither age nor sex, and plundering wherever they had an opportunity. Bodies of women and children were found frightfully mutilated, and at Mr. Wagner's house a woman was found still alive, who bore thirty-seven *assegai* wounds on her body. The movements of the main Zulu army were mysterious.

One day scouts arrived with the information that the enemy was in force between the Tugela and Ekowe; another day information was received that there was an army beyond the later place. The plan adopted on our side was simply to entrench and wait. A dull, monotonous round of garrison duty had to be performed at a number of posts, while the danger was so great and imminent as to turn every citizen into a soldier, and every town into a barrack. As a specimen of life at a fort, we quote from a correspondent who writes in February from "Helpmakaar:"

"Here we are, foot artillery, police, and contingent, about 600 strong, living in tents during the day and going into the fort at night. With the exception of a stink of rotten *mealies* and the rain continually swelling through and through, the fort is not so bad, being so strong and well built that the men here now could hold it against the whole of the Zulu army. It is not healthy. Hospital leaks. What with guards, *vedettes*, etc., the duties are very heavy."

What was said at Helpmakaar might have been said with very little variation at every other fort. The most active operations were carried on from Colonel Wood's column, whose headquarters were entrenched at Kambula. Among its brilliant exploits was the capture, on the 20th February, of the almost inaccessible Makkatees Mountain. One of the captured natives said that our troops had not come a day too soon, as Cetywayo had promised to send reinforcements. The first ship to arrive with reinforcements was H.M.S. *Shah*, which anchored at Port Natal on Thursday, the 6th of March.

The troops available by her were 392 men of the Naval Brigade and 200 men from the St. Helena garrison,[12] Baker and Lonsdale's Light Horse, as well as other irregulars, were recruited in the Cape Colony, and sent on by degrees. The first steamer from England to

---

12. The excellent conduct of Governor Janisch, of St. Helena, in despatching troops in H.M.S. *Shah* to Natal so soon as he received intelligence of the Isandhlwana disaster, forma the subject of a special despatch of thanks and appreciation from the Right Hon. the Secretary of State for the Colonies.

arrive with reinforcements was the *Pretoria*, of the Union Royal Mail Steam Shipping Company's fleet. She made the run to Natal in less than twenty-four days, and had on board 34 officers, 7 staff officers, and 890 men of the 71st Highlanders. The British soldiers were received in Natal with the utmost enthusiasm, as saviours of the country. Each ship and each regiment was eagerly looked for and gladly welcomed. Previous to the *Pretoria*, the 57th Regiment had arrived from Ceylon in H.M. troopship *Tamar*.

The Secretary of War telegraphed, on the 13th of February, to Lord Chelmsford that the following reinforcements had been placed under immediate orders for Natal:—Two regiments of cavalry, each 648 men and 480 horses; two field batteries of artillery, 836 men and 220 horses; one field company of Engineers; five regiments of infantry from home, each 806 men; 57th Regiment from Ceylon; three companies Army Reserve Corps, 140 men, 380 horses; Army Hospital Corps, 140; drafts for the 57th, the 24th, and Royal Artillery. The steamers employed to bring out these troops were—

	Line.	Troops conveyed.
The *Pretoria*	Union S.S. Co.	91st Highlanders
Danube	Ditto	200 men 60th Rifles
Dublin Castle	D. Currie & Co.	3rd Battalion, Rifle Brigade
England	National S.S. Co.	17th Lancers and horses
France	Ditto	Ditto
Egypt	Ditto	1st Dragoon Guards and horses
Spain	Ditto	Ditto
Loando	British and African S.S.Co	Military stores and field telegraph
Russia	Cunard Line	58th Regiment
China	Ditto	94th Regiment
Olympos	Ditto	Royal Artillery
Palmyra	Ditto	Royal Engineers
Manora	McNeil Denny	M Battery, 6th Brigade, Royal Horse Artillery
City of Paris[13]	Inman Company	21st Regiment
City of Venice	Smith & Sons	Army Service and Hospital Corps
Clyde	Temperley's	Drafts of 24th Regiment. Wrecked off Cape Coast, brought in by *Tamar*
Queen Margaret	Queen Line	Army Service Corps and horses

---

13. The *City of Paris* touched the Roman Rock, in Simon's Bay; the Tamar had to take on her troops.

| *Andean* | East India and | |
| | Pacific | Reserve ammunition column |

Major-General Marshall; 1 brigade major; 1 A.D.C.
Major-General Crealock.   *Ditto.*
Major-General Newdigate.   *Ditto.*

These magnificent steamships used the utmost despatch, and in little more than twenty days[14] from England each one arrived at the Cape of Good Hope. The voyage thence to Natal only occupies three days. Immense enthusiasm prevailed as each noble steamer and well-known regiment arrived. The landing at D'Urban was performed in the most expeditious manner, and without the slightest accident. In the midst of all these arrivals and the excitement connected with them, apprehensions of Zulu inroads were at an end; but it was felt that the retrieval of the disaster at Islandhlwana would be a serious work, and that energy and ability were requisite to bring the war to a speedy and satisfactory termination.

The 12th of March was observed throughout the colony of Natal as a day of humiliation, and in every church prayers were offered up to the God of battles, that He would bless our arms. The people of Natal had, in proportion to their numbers, sent out a considerable force across the Tugela. There was mourning in many families for sons, brothers, husbands, slain at Isandhlwana; and the losses caused to sugar estates and other interests by the war were neither small nor unimportant. The war was entirely an imperial act—levied by the High Commissioner, and carried on in Zululand for the protection of the Transvaal and of British South Africa generally, as well as of Natal.

When transport prices increased in accordance with the inexorable laws of supply and demand, immense sums were obtained by wagoners as well as by owners of oxen and wagons. Other classes also greatly benefited by the large military expenditure. It stands to reason that very large sums of money spent in South Africa must have permeated through all classes of the community. At the same time, it is incorrect to charge the people with special greed and rapacity. They have been libelled by more than one person; and with reference to various charges, the Rev. Mr. de Witt, at an early stage of the war, publicly stated in London that the people of Natal treated the Zulus worse than dogs, while, at a subsequent period, Mr. Archibald Forbes,

---

14. The *Manora* made the passage to Simon's Bay in 19 days, 23 hours. Her average speed was 13·5 miles per hour.

correspondent of the *Daily News*, maligned them in the most insulting manner.

It is so well known as to be beyond question that the Zulus are extremely well-treated—too well-treated frequently—by the colonists; and to those conversant with the subject, the missionary's statement at once is seen in its true light, as a mere attempt to obtain a little popularity by joining the usual successful outcry against the oppression of coloured races by the "cruel white men," so constantly echoed by people who have never lived among blacks, and are perfectly ignorant of the facts of the case. Philanthropy obtained at this price, and by means of calumnies against our fellow-countrymen at a distance and in a most trying position of danger, cannot be estimated at a high price. Mr. Forbes was so very short a time in Natal as to be perfectly incompetent to judge of the entire character of the people. His sweeping condemnations must be attributed to bad temper, occasioned by petty inconveniences or rudeness; but it is a pity that a man of his eminence and ability should permit such considerations to affect his judgment or guide his pen.

The fact is that the people of the colonies, and of Natal very especially, are, in proportion to their number, quite superior to the people of Europe. There is more education and more intelligence; consequently, quite as much honesty. Let any man who is really qualified to speak by a real knowledge of the colonies say whether or not this is the truth. Of course, it must be admitted that there is a greater spirit of independence and more freedom, with less conventionality; but this is merely a sequence of the circumstances in which colonists are necessarily placed.

Intelligent and influential public writers in England have gone so far as to assert that "it would not be safe to rely on the energetic co-operation of the Cape," His Excellency the Governor and High Commissioner thus disposes of this subject:—

I fear that possibly, in the press of work, I may have omitted to do justice to the patriotic and energetic spirit shown by the Cape ministry, who in this respect represent, I believe, very faithfully the feeling of the colony generally.

The Cape Government, indeed, appears to me to have done all and much more than could have been expected from it. It has spared a regiment and a half of her Majesty's forces, taken its own recently subdued rebellious districts entirely under its own charge, and is sending to Natal very useful contingents of volunteers, native levies, wagon drivers, supplies of arms, and means of transport in mules, horses, etc.

The tone and spirit generally shown by the Cape Government and people will naturally be compared with that shown by the sister colony of Natal, whose interests are so much greater; and without any reflection on Natal, the population of which has risen to the occasion, the comparison will be by no means un-favourable to the Cape.

It must not be forgotten that the nearer we approach the seat of war, actual or threatened, the greater will be the natural dis-inclination of colonists to volunteer for any but home service, and to leave their houses defenceless. This is, I feel sure, the principal reason of any disinclination to encourage volunteer-ing for service in Zululand; and the threatened disturbance in Basutoland will naturally disincline the Cape colonists to weak-en too far their own means of defence.

The services of the navy during the entire war were of the utmost value. In a despatch dated the 15th of February, the High Commis-sioner brings specially to the notice of her Majesty's Government the excellent service performed by the naval brigades landed from H.M.S. *Active* and *Tenedos* by Admiral Sullivan, and subsequently from the *Boadicea*, These men, in arduous and prolonged military operations, earned most thoroughly the title of "bravest of the brave." No sailor ever turned his back on an enemy during the war, and it was with difficulty that their impetuous heroism could be checked. The *Active* men helped to win the battle of Ineyezane, and were with Colonel Pearson at Ekowe; Fort Tenedos was manned by the men of the ship of that name. This important fort commanded the crossing of the Tugela River near its mouth. Men-of-war cruising on the coast produced an excellent effect, but it is the services of the gallant "blue jackets" in the field which are specially deserving of eulogium.

So soon as the news of the Isandhlwana disaster had been received at St. Helena, Governor Janisch obtained the consent of the military and naval authorities to send off at once every available man to Natal. This was done with promptitude. And the first real ray of sunshine from home reached our troops in Zululand when they heard that 650 gallant men in H.M.S. *Shah*, Captain Bradshaw, had arrived in Natal to assist them.

CHAPTER 6

Relief of Ekowe

It is now necessary to refer to the operations of Colonel Wood's column.

On the 27th of March a force started from the Kambula camp to attack the Zlobane Mountain, consisting of detachments of the Frontier Light Horse, Raaff's Corps, Weatherley's Rangers, Baker's Horse, Major Tremlett with rocket tube, and the *burgher* force. The number of horsemen was 400, and in addition a large body of the Native Contingent was sent, under Major Leet, 1-13th, and Lieutenant Williams, 58th Regiment. Another column was despatched, consisting of mounted infantry, Kaffrarian Mounted Rifles, and Wood's Irregulars, under Commandant Schermbrucker. Colonel Wood, chief in command, and staff followed. We will go with the first column under Colonel Buller, which halted at noon on the south side of the Zinquin Neck. Colonel Weatherley, with his troopers, arrived half an hour afterwards. As the column passed the south side of the Zlobane mountain, two shots were tired from an elephant gun, and three fires were instantaneously lit on a shelf of rock near the summit.

Commandant Uys, a brave Dutch *burgher*, who had already frequently distinguished himself in the war, acted as guide, and the march onward took place in perfect silence. Moving forward in the stillness of death, the east side of the mountain was reached. As the time of action approached, the front post of danger and of honour was taken by Commandant Uys, Colonel Buller, Majors Leet and Tremlett. When 500 yards from the top, the enemy opened a furious fire, in which Lieutenant Williams was killed; but our gallant fellows pressed on without faltering for an instant, and gained the top of the mountain, although the ascent was extremely steep and trying.

The fight continued at this point for another hour, and during the entire time the British force was exposed to a most galling fire from Zulus stationed behind rocks and in caves. When Colonel Wood was within 100 feet from the summit, Mr, Lloyd, his interpreter, fell mortally wounded, and his own horse was shot under him. Colonel Weatherley was desired to dislodge one or two Zulus who were causing most of the loss; but as his men did not advance rapidly.

Captain Campbell, Lieutenant Lysons, and three men of the 90th, jumping over a low wall, ran forward and charged into a cave, where Captain (the Hon. B.) Campbell, leading in the most gallant and determined manner, was shot dead. Lieutenant Lysons and Private Fowler followed closely on his footsteps, and one of them, for each shot fired, killed one Zulu and dislodged another, who crawled away by a subterraneous passage, reappearing higher up the mountain.

After silencing the fire of the Zulus at the top of the Zlobane mountain. Colonel Buller and Commandant Raaff rode to the westward end, where the track divides it. The Zulus had fortified the pass with stone walls, and from this position were annoying the rear of the attacking force. In the meantime parties of Raaff's and Baker's Horse, and the *burgher* force, kept up a hot fire on the enemy lurking under the *krantzes* on the north-west side, where the Zulu troops had built huts for encampment.

After having been four or five hours on the summit, Colonel Buller, with Commandments Uys and Raaff, were returning from silencing the enemy's fire at the pass, when they noticed the arrival of a body of Zulus on the northern extremity of the mountain. Colonel Buller rode off to attack them, but before he could get half-way, he saw that troops of natives were climbing every available baboon-path, with the object of cutting off the retreat of our men from the only two passes by which it was possible to descend. At the same time, two great columns of the enemy were seen approaching along the top of the mountain to the eastward, and another dense mass of men advancing from the southward. Colonel Bullet then gave the order to ride for the pass over the *krantz* at the neck, which was the only exit left open.

Then ensued a scene which almost defies description, Down a descent fearfully steep and covered with boulders horses were ridden at full speed. Many who lost their steeds were saved on the cruppers of their comrades. At the foot, Colonel Boiler, with other officers, did everything possible to rally sufficient men to cover the retreat of those still descending, but every effort was in vain. The retreat became a flight, and that even degenerated into a species of stampede, panic guiding the actions of the fugitives. It was when endeavouring to descend the mountain that the brave Commandant Uys was killed. He had already reached such a forward position as to be comparatively free from danger, when he learned that one of his sons was behind, and might probably fall into the enemy's hands. He returned immediately, but only to die. A ring of savages closed around him.

True to the traditions of his race, he fought bravely to the last, and only succumbed to overwhelming force. He fell, stabbed to death by numerous *assegais*. The family of Piet Uys was celebrated in Kafir wars. He was born in the Humansdorp district of the Cape Colony, and his family left that neighbourhood for Natal in 1837. Both his father and brother were killed fighting against Dingaan, and he himself, determining to avenge their death, was among the first to offer his services. In one of his letters he writes, "I fight in a good faith and a righteous cause. I must avenge the death of my father and brother, although in doing so I am almost sure to lose my life; yet I cannot restrain myself when I remember how they were slain."

A similar fate was reserved for the gallant Colonel Weatherley. This officer, with his Rangers, delayed starting in retreat, and lost his way. Nearly every man of his force was cut off, while their brave leader, holding his son—a boy of fourteen—to his breast, fought manfully, until he fell pierced with numerous wounds.

Thus perished two of the most gallant officers who served in the war—one of Dutch extraction, the other an Englishman. The services of Commandant Uys were of such great value, in consequence of his bravery and thorough knowledge of the country, as to receive special recognition, and no more gallant officer fought under the British flag than poor Weatherley, of the Transvaal Rangers.

Among those killed at the Zlobane was a man named Calverley, whose antecedents were of a very peculiar and somewhat suspicious character. He had come as ambassador from Oham, the brother of Cetywayo, by whom he was evidently completely trusted. Shuffling and vacillation characterized the negotiations, and it was noticed in camp that Calverley rode the horse on which Lieutenant Coghill was killed at Isandhlwana. He likewise possessed property known to have been lost in that disaster. But for strict military discipline, Calverley would undoubtedly have been killed by our soldiers, and even after Oham came over he was still treated with suspicion. On this day, however, be expiated any faults be may have committed by his blood, and died fighting in the British ranks against the enemies of Oham and of England.

Colonel Wood was riding slowly under the Zlobane Mountain to the westward, perfectly unconscious of the existence of a large Zulu force moving on the left across his front. When about half-way, at the centre of the mountain, one of the natives, named Umtanga, explained by signs that a large Zulu army was close upon them. From an adjacent bill they perceived that a great host was inarching towards them, disposed in five columns, with horns and the usual dense "chest," in accordance with the rule of formation for attack.

An order was sent to Colonel Russell, who was then ascending the western end of the range, to move eastward and cover the movement of our natives to the camp. At 7 p.m. Colonel Wood reached camp. Intelligence came in that Captain Barton's party were on foot about ten miles distant, and Colonel Buller at once started in heavy rain, and was able by means of led horses to bring in seven men, who were the sole survivors of the Border Horse and of Captain Barton's party. Thus terminated this disastrous affair, in which our loss amounted to about 120 men, and in which the enemy gained additional courage for the great attack on the camp so shortly to follow.

Captain D'Arcy, of Irregular Horse, thus briefly and forcibly sums up his experience of Zlobane:—

Now to give you a short account. Three hundred and fifty of the mounted men had to take a very strong position, a hill called the Zlobane. We got up there, driving the natives back at every point, although they fought very well. Williams was killed as we charged up the hill, the baron on the top when he was in command of his troop; a Zulu spotted him from a hole, right through his head. Barton was sent down a hill with some of C Troop, and just as we got down we saw about 20,000 Zulus below us, trying to get between us and the camp.

We at once crossed the hill to come down a most fearfully steep place; the Dutchmen got to the place, rushed down, and bolted as hard as they could go. My troop was leading, and Blaine, myself, and Hutton got them to go quietly down the hill, which was really a fearful place. I had, of course, to stop on the top of the hill, as we were retreating; the Zulus all this time were giving us awful pepper from Martini rifles. I saw, I thought, all our men down, and then considered I had to think of myself.

I got half-way down, when a stone about the size of a small

piano came bounding down. I heard a shout above, 'Look out below,' and down the beastly thing came right on my horse's leg, cutting it right off. I at the same time got knocked down the hill by another horse, and was nearly squeezed to death. I had taken the bridle off, and was about to take the saddle (I mean I was going up the hill to take it off my horse), when I heard a scream; I looked up, and saw the Zulus right in among the white men, stabbing horses and men, I made a jump for it, and got down somehow or other, and ran as hard as I could with seventy rounds of ball cartridge, a carbine, revolver, field-glass, and heavy boots.

I went some 300 yards, when a fellow called Francis got a horse for me, but no saddle or bridle—a rein did for both; when one of the Frontier Light Horse got wounded through the leg, and I had to jump off, put him on my horse, and run again. Colonel Buller saved my life by taking me up behind him on his horse; then Blaine, who had been keeping the natives off in the rear, saw me (as after I got my breath I got off the colonel's horse), and he nearly cried when he met me, all the fellows thinking I had been killed on the top of the hill. He behaved as he always does, and stuck to me, and pulled me through the second time.

The third time a major in the artillery, Tremlett by name, took me up behind. Our men and officers all behaved well, but the other volunteers were what Major Robinson would call a big rabble. We lost ninety-three white men and a number of natives. The Frontier Light Horse lost three officers and twenty-four non-commissioned officers and men, and sixty-six horses. Each of our men arrived in camp with another man behind him.

The great Zulu army which nearly succeeded in encircling Colonel Wood's mounted party at the Zlobane Mountain, was discerned from the Kambula camp at 9 a.m. on the 29th of March. Flushed with the success of the previous day, and depending on their vast number and excellent organization, they had determined to sweep away forever the small white force which had entrenched itself in their midst. For four hours the Zulu army continued to advance at a slow pace, executing the manoeuvres considered necessary to surround Kambula. The left horn was seen marching in the direction of Balter Spruit for over three hours before the men of the right horn made their appearance.

About 1 p.m. the enemy began to make a rapid advance to the right of the Kambula hill, facing Blood River. It was then time to prepare. Orders were given to eat dinners with haste. The alarm sounded, tents were lowered, positions were taken up on and underneath the wagons, boxes of ammunition were opened, and every preparation for defence was promptly made.

When the right horn of the Zulu army was within two miles distance, a mounted party went out amidst hearty cheers to give them battle. Having advanced and fired, the enemy became too numerous, and our men retired, drawing the Zulus after them, which was the real object of this manoeuvre. The right horn of the enemy's army then commenced its attack in earnest, pressing on most bravely in spite of a tremendous fire from the artillery, the 90th Light Infantry, and the 1-13th. Shell ploughed their ranks, but they re-formed and steadily came on. At last, chiefly through the scathing fire of shot and shell from four of our big guns, the movements of the enemy became paralyzed, and a panic commenced. At the rear of the *laager* a body of the Zulus had gained the top of the hill, about 300 yards off, and kept up a galling fire upon the men of the 13th Regiment.

All, however, was soon over, the Zulus wavered, hesitated, turned, and fled. Amidst lusty cheers our men followed in pursuit. F and G Companies of the 13th charged them down the ravine at the point of the bayonet. Shrapnel, case shot, etc., continued to pour from the field-pieces on the heavy masses of disorganized Zulus. The cavalry for seven miles pursued them, until it was too dark to see. Many were shot down at distances of ten and fifteen yards, while hand-to-hand encounters with the flying foe diversified the scene.

The strength of the Zulu army at Kambula exceeded 20,000, and their plan of battle was evidently to advance the right horn of their army so as to entice our troops to come out and attack it. The left horn would then have advanced up the ravine, and gaining the summit of the hill, charge and take possession of the wagons, thus completely surrounding our position. In fact, the Isandhlwana tactics were to be repeated. Fortunately, however, the lesson we learned there was not in vain, and Kambula proved this to demonstration. The Native Contingent ran away before the fight, but the Basutos stood steadily at their posts and fought well.

The flower of Cetywayo's army, consisting of young unmarried men, was engaged in this attack, and more than 1200 were slain. No fewer than 786 bodies of Zulus were buried in the immediate vicinity of the camp. It is noteworthy that they had many kinds of breechloaders—Martini, Snider, and Mitford's patterns being all represented. It was a grand sight to see the great moving mass of more than 20,000 Zulu warriors advancing straight amidst a withering fire. They shouted out when near the camp, "We are the boys from Isandhlwana," and retreated under circumstances where no European forces in the world could have advanced. The victory was specially one of artillery. The first shot was fired at 1.25 p.m., and the last at 6.25 p.m. Three hundred and sixty-two shells and eighty-six charges of canister were expended.

Many acts of gallantry were performed. Colonel Wood, as usual, was pre-eminent. The bravery and coolness of Captain Woodgate was the subject of admiration, while Colonel Buller greatly added to the laurels be had so deservedly earned in the retreat from the Zlobane Mountain. It was on the latter occasion that he six times risked his life in carrying out of danger and saving six men who, being unhorsed, must otherwise have fallen into the bands of a remorseless and savage foe. Thirty killed and fifty wounded was the loss on our side at the battle of Kambula.

A description of the repulse of the Zulus from Kambula camp has been written by Commandant Schermbrucker, and this is what he says:—

As soon as we saw them turning their backs, I got all my Kaffirarians rapidly to mount the horses already saddled, and shortly afterwards all the mounted forces in camp were ready, and we raced helter-skelter after the flying Zulus. I took the extreme right. Colonel Buller led the centre, and Colonel Russell, with mounted infantry, took the left. For fully seven miles I chased two columns of the enemy, who tried to escape over the Umvolozi, but I came beforehand and pushed them off the road. They fairly ran like bucks; but I was after them like the whirlwind, and shooting incessantly into the thick column, which could not have been less than 6000 strong. They became exhausted, and shooting them down would have taken too much time; so we took the *assegais* from the dead men, and rushed among the living ones, stabbing them right and left, with fearful revenge for the misfortunes of the 28th inst. No quarter was given.

On the 12th of March a very serious disaster occurred at the Intombe River, where an escort of the 80th Regiment, under Captain

72

Moriarty, was *laagered*. That officer commanded a party of 104 men convoying a train of eighteen wagons variously loaded, *en route* from Derby to Luneberg. The flooded state of the river caused detention for several days. A small party under Lieutenant Harward was stationed on the other side. That officer heard a shot fired at 4 a.m., and shortly afterwards was roused by an alarm, and saw, when the fog lifted, a dense mass of Zulus, about 4000 in number, extending across the valley and on the point of surprising the camp on the other side of the river. He immediately put his men, thirty-five in number, under arms, and directed their fire on the flanks of the enemy.

With tremendous celerity. Captain Moriarty's force was surprised and the camp taken. An immediate retreat was made by Harward, but not before the awful sight was witnessed of the enemy slaughtering our men on the banks of the river and in the water. The Zulus crossed and came on in dense masses. A hand-to-hand fight ensued, and a vain attempt to rally was made; then, finding re-formation impossible. Lieutenant Harward put spurs to his horse and galloped into Luneberg. Forty-four men were killed.

An eyewitness, Mr. Josiah Sussons, says;—

I was in the wagon, sleeping, and early in the morning I got up to see if it was daylight, and saw the Kafirs swarming around within twenty yards of me. The alarm was given, and Captain Moriarty called out, 'Guards out.' I ran back to my wagon to get my rifle (which belonged to No. 1 Company, Transvaal Rifle Volunteers, of which corps I am a member), but in the confusion of the bullets flying about me, I could not get it out. I now found it so dangerous that I determined to try to bolt, if I could, without remaining to take my clothes.

As I emerged from the wagon for the last time, I heard Captain Moriarty cry out, 'Fire away, men; I am done.' I then went to the adjoining wagon to call Whittington (also a Pretoria man), and I told him the niggers were around. He immediately came out and jumped down, but was caught almost as soon as he got to the ground, and *assegaied*. The poor fellow shrieked out, but without avail, as no assistance was at hand.

Seeing that I was powerless to do anything, having no arms of any kind, I ran down between the oxen, and made for the river, which was about sixty yards off. I found the Zulus shooting and stabbing the people in all directions. The sight was a most horrifying one, and never to be forgotten. I had to dodge about to save myself, and am surprised that I managed to get through at all. As soon as I got to the river, I jumped in and made a dive, as swimming was too dangerous, the Zulus standing on the banks, and at the edge of the river, as thick as thieves, throwing *assegais* and aiming their guns wherever they saw a head.

I came up about the middle of the river, but the moment my head was out, I saw several Zulus pointing their guns, and ready to file. I therefore dived again, and came out on the other side. The river was very full at the time, and a strong current running. In crossing I had torn off my shirt, the only garment I possessed, and therefore when I landed I was entirely in a state of nudity. I now found that fighting was still going on on all sides of me, and that it was almost impossible I could get any further, and in my desperation I contemplated throwing myself in the water, to be drowned peaceably, rather than suffer the death by torture of many of those I saw around me.

I, however, got into a courageous spirit again, and dashed off, keeping as much out of the way of the enemy as I could. Several shots were fired at me, and *assegais* were flying in all directions, but somehow I happened to be fortunate and got clear of the encampment. I made for Meyer's station as fast as I could, and overtook one soldier on the road, who was shot dead just as I got up to him. I overtook two others shortly after, who were also shot. Getting farther on, I fell in with Sergeant Booth and about a dozen men, who were keeping up a retreating fire, and fighting very pluckily.

I rested for a few minutes with them, during which time I espied the Zulus coming round the hill to intercept us. I informed Sergeant Booth of this, and he kept up a steady fire upon them, and made the enemy retire back into the hills. I cannot speak too highly of the conduct of Sergeant Booth on this occasion; he fought most pluckily, and lost four of his small band here. It was entirely owing to their doing so well that any of us managed to get through at all. The Zulus would have entirely surrounded us, and not a soul could have escaped. Seventeen leaders and drivers were killed altogether, amongst them being Whittington, Campbell, and Goss. As I got in camp, I met Major Tucker going out with his men to the relief.

One of the most sensational events which occurred during April at the headquarters camp of the fourth (Colonel Wood's) column, was the arrival there of a man whose hairbreadth escapes enable us to realize that truth is stranger than fiction. Captain Mayne Reid could scarcely venture on imagining what our readers will find stated below as sober fact. There may be exaggeration or colouring, but in the main the narrative is correct. Mr. Rudolph, *landrost* of Utrecht, when out scouting on the Zunguin Neck with five men, encountered a party of forty Zulus, of whom be killed four. He picked up about the same time a Frenchman named Grandier, who had belonged to Colonel Weatherley's troop of Border Horse, and was made prisoner by the enemy when so many of his comrades fell at the Zlobane Mountain. The story was told to Colonel Wood and the staff—Captain Maude taking notes, the substance of which is as follows:—

He (Grandier) was one of the very few who succeeded in charging through the mass of Zulus by whom they were beset in front and rear. He had got on to fairly good ground, and had set a comrade on his horse, he running by the side, when a Kafir caught him by the leg, and he was immediately overpowered by numbers and made prisoner. His captors took him to Umbellini's *kraal*, on the south side of the Zlobane, about half-way up. He saw that chief, who asked him where Shepstone was, and who was the commander of the commando to which he belonged.

He was kept prisoner that night in a *kraal*, and sent out the next morning to work in the *mealie* fields. Soon after he was taken by two or three mounted men to the middle of a big commando, all of whom threatened him with death, while the chief, Manymane, ordered him to be sent prisoner to Cetywayo. He stopped one day after that at the Zlobane, starting the next day for Ulundi in charge of four men riding, while he was made to walk and carry their provisions. He was quite naked, all his clothes having been taken from him. They took four days to make the journey, arriving in the evening, when a messenger was sent forward to announce their coming to the king. He remained all that night and next day tied in a field.

On the following day, at noon, he was taken to Cetywayo, where a half-caste Dutchman, with long hair, translated. Cetywayo asked what the English wanted coming in that way to his country. He asked after Oham, where he was stopping, and said he would kill him and Shepstone and everyone else, as he had plenty of men to do the work. He was very particular to learn the name of the commander of the Kambula column. After replying to these questions, Grandier was removed in custody to, a *kraal*, where he was threatened and beaten with very little respite, and for four days had nothing but *mealies* to eat.

Some messengers then came and reported to Cetywayo that Umbellini and his brother had been killed in the attack on Colonel Wood's camp. On this Cetywayo ordered Grandier to be sent back to Umbellini's Kafirs, that they might sacrifice him to the *manes* of their deceased chief. He was sent back next day with a guard of two Zulus, only one of whom had a gun, though plentifully supplied with *assegais*.

On the 13th, about noon, they were resting, after a long tramp, and the Zulus being sleepy, Grandier watched his opportunity, snatched an *assegai*, and pinned one man to the earth; the other woke up in a fright and ran for his life. Grandier then made off in the direction of the camp, walking all night and steering a course by the stars, when this morning he was seen by Mr. Rudolph's party and brought in, so crippled in the feet that he is at present in hospital. He saw at Ulundi a Portuguese, who makes guns for Cetywayo, and on the morning of the 14th so large a force of Kafirs, driving cattle, passed him that he was obliged to remain hid all the morning to let them pass.

About the beginning of April, everything was at last ready for the relief of Ekowe. Nearly six thousand troops of all arms started from Fort Tenedos, representing almost every branch of the service. The relieving column consisted as follows:—

EKOWE RELIEVING COLUMN.

FIRST DIVISION OF THE COLUMN.

Lieutenant-Colonel Law, R.A., commanding.

	Men
Naval Brigade of H.M.S. *Shah* and *Tenedos*, except the Royal Marines of the *Shah*	350
The 57th Regiment	640
2 companies the "Buffs"	140
5 companies 99th Regiment	430
5th Battalion N.N.C.	1200
Mounted infantry	70
Do. volunteers	40
Do. Natives	130

Native foot scouts	150
Commissariat and transport department	——
Medical department	——
Total	1660 whites
	1480 N.C.
Grand total	3140 fighting men

Artillery— 2 9-pounder guns.

2 24-pounder rocket tubes

1 Gatling gun

There accompanied this division of the column the train of supplies for Ekowe (a month's supply for 1200 men, about 25 wagons); a train of supplies for both divisions of the column for 10 days, about 25 wagons.

SECOND DIVISION OF THE COLUMN.

Lieutenant-Colonel Pemberton, 60th Rifles, commanding.

	Men
Naval Brigade of H.M.S. *Boadicea*	190
Royal Marines, *Shah* and *Boadicea*	100
60th Rifles	540
91st Highlanders	850
4th Battalion N.N.C	800
Commissariat and transport department	—
Medical department	—
Total	1680 whites
	800 N.C.
Total fighting men	2480

Artillery— 2 24-pounder rocket tubes.

1 Gatling gun.

Grand total	1660 whites.	1480 natives.
	1680 do.	800 do.
	3340	2280

Grand total of fighting men   5620

On Saturday, the 30th of March, a start was made at daybreak, and the column halted within entrenchments for the night at Inyoni River. The force advanced without tents, and with only a blanket and waterproof sheet for each man. On Sunday the Amatekulu River was reached, and here a considerable detention took place in consequence of difficulty in crossing. On Tuesday the column reached the hills which border the Inyezane Valley, and then a site was selected for an entrenched *laager*. On this day mounted patrols and scouts of the enemy were seen for the first time. News was then received that a large force was marching down, and that an attack might be expected at any moment. The famous Ginghelovo camp was then constructed. It was made sufficiently large for 2000 cattle to be placed in the centre, trenches were dug, and the wagons laced together according to the approved method.

About eight o'clock on Tuesday evening (2nd April), a false alarm took place, but nothing further noteworthy occurred until daybreak of the next day, when the mounted natives and scouts were sent out. A little before 6 a.m. (Wednesday, 3rd April) our men fell back shooting steadily, and immediately after two large columns of the enemy were seen coming down the Inyezane hills, while one came round the left by the Amatekulu Bush, and another smaller one from the direction of the old military *kraal*. In ten minutes' time the camp was surrounded and the attack commenced. The nature of the ground favoured the enemy, who came up with a rush to a distance of 400 yards; then they scattered and obtained shelter in long grass which grew about the camp.

For one hour and a half, a heavy fusillade was kept up from both sides, and as the Gatlings, two 9-pounder guns, and the rocket tubes were all in action, such a tremendous fire was poured into the enemy as to prevent the possibility of their advancing. Many of our men, firing from wagons and high positions, were able to pick off Zulus with their rifles. This destructive fire evidently had a great effect upon the enemy. At half past seven o'clock, the mounted men and those of the Native Contingent went out amidst tremendous cheering, and drove the Zulus before them from the long grass, and continued the pursuit for a distance of four miles. Masses of the enemy then clustered upon the hills, but dispersed upon being shelled from the fort.

During the action. Lord Chelmsford and his staff went round the trenches, encouraging the men, and telling them to fire steadily and low. The general himself was not mounted, but the members of his staff were. Colonel Crealock received a wound in the arm, and lost a horse; a bullet went through Lieutenant Milne's clothes; and Captain Molyneux had two horses shot under him. No fewer than 778 dead bodies of the enemy were found within a distance of 1000 yards from the fort. A flying column was now formed, consisting of the 57th, 60th, and 91st regiments, with 100 of the Naval Brigade, and a few of John Dunn's scouts. It ought to be mentioned that Dunn had already performed excellent service, and was attached to headquarters as principal guide. The life of this man had been a very peculiar one. Born of English parents in the Cape Colony, he had been brought to Natal, and early in life entered Zululand as a trader. Eventually, he learned the language and adopted the manners and habits of the savages. He was made an *induna* or chief, acquired cattle, wives, and other property, and in many respects became the right-hand councillor and adviser of Cetywayo. This is the more remarkable as he had, previous to that monarch's accession, espoused the cause of his brother.

It is suspected that he made himself peculiarly useful in supplying guns, and in this way gained much of both his influence and his wealth. When war was declared by Britain, he came over with his flocks, herds, and wives, became the trusted adviser and guide of the general in command, and was marked out for preferment and favour. The flying column left at daybreak on Thursday, reached the Inyezane at about eleven, and as the sun was setting came in view of the large hill behind which lay Ekowe. Colonel Pearson galloped out by the new road, with 600 of his men, and when he grasped the hand of Lord Chelmsford felt like one called forth from a dungeon to the cheerful light of the sun. The fort he had guarded so well was relieved. Crushing anxiety and responsibility were succeeded by thankful congratulations. The cloud which hung around Ekowe had passed away.[15]

15. One who was there, writing *in Blackwood's Magazine*, tells us: "On the afternoon of the 3rd (April) the column detailed on the 31st March, about 500 whites and 50 blacks, and the mounted infantry with one gun, left the fort, under General Pearson, to meet the relief column. .A solitary horseman is seen towards 6 p.m., galloping up the new road to the fort: he had an officer's coat on, and we could see a sword dangling from his side. Who is he? He proved to be the correspondent of the *Standard*. 'First in Ekowe,' he said; 'proud to shake hands with an Ekoweian,' A second horseman appeared, approaching the fort, his horse apparently much blown. Who is he? The correspondent of the *Argus* (Cape Town). They had a race who would be first in Ekowe, the *Standard* winning by five minutes. Thus, it was two Press correspondents who distanced everyone and were the first men to arrive." Four officers and twenty-seven men were buried at Ekowe. Two hundred sick officers and men were taken to hospital; Captain Wynne and Lieutenant Thirkell died shortly after.

CHAPTER 7

Review of the Campaign

The Native Contingent, composed of loyal Zulus, although a large force, turned out a comparatively useless one. After the battle of Isandhlwana, Colonel Glynn reports (on the 24th of January), "The whole of the Native Contingent walked off this morning," The reasons for this conduct are furnished elaborately in a minute of Sir H. Bulwer, Lieutenant-Governor of Natal, dated the 29th of January. These men had numerous complaints. On the night of the 23rd of January, whilst the European force at Rorke's Drift was entrenched, the Native Contingent had no such protection. The general and his staff leaving camp exercised a depressing influence. Uncertainty existed regarding their wives and families. These reasons, and reasons such as these, were furnished as explanations for their desertion.

Sir Henry Bulwer had been always of opinion that to do away with the native system of organization for the purpose of substituting a regimental system was one of very doubtful advisableness. Nevertheless, he consented to give the men required, and no fewer than 7050 were sent into the field. Lord Chelmsford declared that he had never been able to understand what the tribal system was, and that as often as he had endeavoured to obtain information he had been baffled by vague generalities and oft-repeated laudations. So anxious, however, were the commandants to carry out what they considered the tribal system, that the companies were organized with uneven strength, in order that men of different tribes should be kept distinct.

Sir Henry Bulwer believed that each column should have had a Native Contingent, and that these should have been led by officers who represented the Lieutenant-Governor, or Supreme Chief. They would have then moved and fought in accordance with their customs. The general could not agree to this. The natives must be divided into battalions 1000 strong, and into companies 100 strong. They were not to fight in their own fashion, and European officers, who did not know their language, were given commands among them. Dissatisfaction, discontent, and inefficiency resulted in such a manner that in all respects the large Native Contingent, numbering more than 7000 men, was a failure.

Later on, very serious differences of opinion arose between Lord Chelmsford and Sir Henry Bulwer. In reply to suggestions from the general, the Executive Council of Natal decided, on the 1st of March, that—

(a.) In the opinion of this Council the proposition that raiding expeditions should be made into the Zulu country by the natives of this colony is unadvisable of adoption, as being an impolitic and undesirable system of war, as being calculated to provoke retaliation, and as tending to demoralize the people engaged in it.

(b.) 1. That the proposition to call out every available native in the colony is open to serious objections.

2. That a large proportion of the able-bodied male population has already been called out, and that this Council considers it undesirable to press the power of the Supreme Chief to a point that would probably cause serious discontent amongst the natives.

3. That all trading, commercial, and farming operations would be thereby disorganized and ruinous consequences would ensue, the natives forming practically the only labouring portion of the population in the upper districts of the colony.

4. That the calling out of the whole able-bodied male population would, in all probability, induce a panic, and be attended with serious inconveniences.

It will thus be seen that very unfortunate differences of opinion existed between the supreme military power and the civil government of Natal. It certainly must be admitted that, as a rule, the friendly Zulus of the colony were of little good as fighting men in the campaign. Whether or not the opposite would have been the case if the dangerous experiment had been tried of allowing them to fight with their own weapons and in their own fashion is extremely doubtful. The tribal system, root and branch, is a failure in Natal, and a constant source of danger and anxiety. So soon, therefore, as by means of enlightened statesmanship it can be completely broken up and destroyed, the better for the protection and defence of the colony, as well as for the cause of civilization and the nation we are trying to civilize.

On the 11th of April, the general, writing to the Secretary of State for War, says:

My orders regarding demonstrations were fully carried out, but the fullness of the Tugela would have prevented any general raid being made, even if the Natal natives had not been forbidden to cross the border by his Excellency the Lieutenant-Governor of Natal.

In order to enable my readers to understand the entire question fully, I subjoin that portion of Sir Henry Bulwer's despatch to the Secretary of State (April 16) which refers to the subject. He says:

I have placed under the command of the lieutenant-general, for service in the Zulu country, the Natal Mounted Police, most of the Natal Mounted Volunteers, a number of natives who have been formed into what is called the Natal Native Contingent, and a number of natives for pioneer, transport, and hospital service, and that I have never interfered with them, nor have I expected that the lieutenant-general's orders to them should be referred to me before being complied with; but with regard to the native levies, which have been called oat for the defence of the colony, and placed under the command of colonial district commanders to protect the border and the colony, I have never placed them in any way, directly or indirectly, under the command of the lieutenant-general for service in the Zulu country, nor have I authorized, directly or indirectly, in any way, their being taken across the border, or their being employed in making raids into the Zulu country.

These levies were called out expressly and solely for service in the colony and for the defence of the colony, and 'were placed under the colonial district commanders for that purpose only. The colonial district commanders were, of course, made subject, so far as regarded the defence of their districts, and the movement and disposition of any forces under them in their districts, to the military command; but no authority has been given, either to these colonial district commanders or to the lieutenant-general, to employ the native levies, which were exclusively called out for the defence of the colony, on any service

82

in the Zulu country, and I submit that the lieutenant-general in issuing any instructions for these native levies to cross the border to make raids into Zulu country, in issuing these instructions as he has done, without my authority, without my concurrence, and positively without any reference to me, has exceeded his powers and acted without a due regard for the authority of this Government.

I pass by the question of the expediency or policy of making raids into the Zulu country. In a letter addressed by me to the High Commissioner, I have ventured to put before his Excellency for his consideration the question of the expediency of such a policy, and the risks involved in such a course, namely, the risk of retaliation, and the risk of irritating and alienating unnecessarily those of the Zulu people who might otherwise be disposed to come to friendly terms with us, and through whose friendly disposition towards as a satisfactory solution of the difficulties between us and the Zulu people might eventually be more easily arrived at. But I do not claim to have any authority in respect of this question, and I have done no more than venture to lay my suggestion before the High Commissioner, and to forward a copy of my letter to the lieutenant-general.

With regard to the employment of the native levies who had been called up for the defence of the border on service beyond the border and in making raids, I have already shown that the levies to which I refer were never in any way placed under the lieutenant-general for employment across the border; and I have also shown that they were levies which have nothing whatsoever to do with the Native Contingent battalions to which the lieutenant-general refers as having been hitherto associated with the British troops, and which were placed under his command for service across the border.

The question, therefore, put by the lieutenant-general, in the way that it is put before the Secretary of State for War, by not distinguishing between the two descriptions of native forces, but, as is actually done in the last paragraph but one, by naming and associating the two together as if there were no distinction between them, fails, I think, to represent the real state of the case.

The general in command had felt extremely what he considered the absence of co-operation on the part of Sir Henry Bulwer. Writing to the Secretary of State for War on the 11th of April, Lord Chelmsford mentions that when he had determined to move up to Ekowe, secret instructions were sent to the different commanders along the border from the Lower Tugela up to Kambula Hill, requesting them to make strong demonstrations all along the line, and, if possible, to raid into Zululand. At this juncture the Lieutenant-Governor forbade the Natal natives to cross.

A general raid into Zululand effected by a large body of native troops would, in the opinion of Lord Chelmsford, have produced very important results, and the general strongly resents the interference of Sir H. Bulwer with his plans. The quarrel—for it was nothing less—to which allusion has now been made, was very probably one of the reasons for the appointment of Sir Garnet Wolseley, who in his own person united both supreme civil and supreme military power.

In the Zulu war there were two campaigns—the first ended in Isandhlwana, the second at Ulundi. Between these battles there was an immense interval, chiefly occupied in moving great masses of men and greater masses of supplies to the front. Lord Chelmsford is blamed for want of foresight and care in the first campaign, want of energy and judgment in the second campaign, and want of generalship in both. There are two sides to the case, and it is necessary to advert to both. Great difficulties were in the way; but until the arrival of Sir Garnet Wolseley raid the joyful day of Ulundi, it must be admitted that the general did not conquer obstacles, but obstacles conquered him.

Let us endeavour to view the general conduct of the first campaign in the light of facts about which there can be no question. Early in January Lord Chelmsford was at the head of an army sufficiently numerous and powerful for the conquest of Zululand. We shall see that at Ulundi 4000 soldiers, properly handled, were adequate to the complete defeat of 20,000 Zulus, comprising the flower of Cetywayo's army; therefore it is absurd to imagine that, if good generalship had been used, any defeat could have been sustained in the first advance. Colonel Pearson was thoroughly victorious at Inyezane, and Colonel Wood was also successful. Disastrous failure, however, overtook the column of the general-in-chief.

Lord Chelmsford, conducting a large force with enormous stores, made Rorke's Drift on the Tugela his base of operations, and subsequently was forced to trust to the extraordinary efforts of a young Engineer officer for the safety of Natal. All experience of Zulu warfare had shown the absolute necessity of entrenchments, yet the central column marched into Zululand without constructing a single breastwork. The personal safety of the commander-in-chief and that of half his column became really due to a sudden inspiration and to a happy accident. Young subalterns conceived and carried a plan of defence where *mealie*-bags formed the breastworks and biscuit-boxes the entrenchments. It was providential that such officers as Chard and Bromhead were there to do the work.

Lord Chelmsford was woefully deficient in knowledge of the enemy's movements. An immense army lay in wait to destroy his camp while he, with scattered forces, pursued a Will-o'-the-wisp foe which found do difficulty in luring him on to destruction. He had mounted men, but does not seem to have used them efficiently as scouts. Colonel Buller, the able head of his intelligence branch, was in quite another part of the country. Lord Chelmsford either completely despised the enemy, which was a blunder in itself, or he was incapable of appreciating his real position, and of taking the evident means of preserving the column under his charge. He evidently wanted that genius or instinct so absolutely necessary to constitute a great military leader. A really great general, like a poet, is born, not made; and it was the misfortune of the British army not to have secured one on this important occasion.

No entrenchment or *laager* was either made or ordered to be made at Isandhlwana, although it must be admitted that if the general had been as lucky in subordinates there as at Rorke's Drift, a very different issue of the day would have been the result. Nothing could surpass the madness of Colonel Durnford in scattering his troops at the very moment when, by means of laagering, or at least forming a hollow square, it would have been possible to resist the attack of the enemy. It is a libel on our soldiers to hint that they did not behave well. The short service system is in no way responsible for the disaster.

The gallant 24th, as well as the other troops, fought with the utmost bravery, and, if they had been commanded by such a man as Wood or Pearson, undoubtedly would have gained a brilliant victory. A few hundred Dutchmen, without breech-loading guns, had behind a rough fortification of wagons defied an entire Zulu army. Chard and Bromhead, with 100 infantry soldiers, at the back of *mealie*-bags and biscuit-boxes, were able to drive back immensely superior forces. It is therefore preposterous to imagine that our troops at Isandhlwana, assisted by well-served large guns, could not easily, if properly commanded, have been able to hold their own, at least until the rest of the column arrived.

In ten days' time Lord Chelmsford was so unfortunate as to sustain a most signal defeat, in which half his force was literally butchered, and his large quantity of ammunition and stores captured by the enemy. His flank was turned and his column surprised by an army of naked savages, without artillery, about whose movements his ignorance was as profound as it was surprising. A similar success to that gained by Colonel Pearson would have virtually concluded the war. A march to Ulundi by a strong flying column would have been possible, and Great Britain might then have saved the blood of many of her best soldiers, and fully three million pounds sterling of her treasure.

The opinions now expressed are those of the majority of military correspondents and military men, but the thorough novelty and difficulty of operations do not seem sufficiently taken into account. Besides, in judging Lord Chelmsford, it must be specially remembered that his instructions about concentrating at Isandhlwana camp were not attended to, and to this fact many attributed the disaster that ensued. Certainly no one deserved sympathy more than this general, whose misfortunes were quite as great as his faults. Subsequently, he did everything in his power to make the campaign successful. Reinforcements poured in, and were pushed forward to the front. It is true that delays occurred, but these, it is argued, were thoroughly unsurmountable.

We shall find at last that Lord Chelmsford finished the campaign with glory and success at the great battle of Ulundi. The people of Natal and the Cape Colony, who had sympathized with his reverses, thoroughly recognized the greatness of this victory and rejoiced in his triumph. It is only fair, when furnishing opinions full of condemnation, to refer at the same time to the fact that contrary views are held by numerous men of intelligence, who have had every opportunity of studying the subject.

The disaster of Isandhlwana was pregnant with results almost too awful to contemplate. Natal was panic-stricken. Twenty thousand white people were threatened, not only with the victorious army, but with hundreds of thousands of natives, kept heathen and alien from motives of policy, who would have, out of fear of Cetywayo, quickly joined any army of massacre which that tyrant could have sent to devastate Natal. Fortunately, in spite of their much-vaunted strategy, the Zulus proved unequal to the task of taking advantage of their victory. Had they, in the first instance, only allowed the general to move forward into his new camp, the destruction of the column could have been made complete. It was by a miracle that Lord Chelmsford and the men with him escaped. If they had been attacked when, exhausted and dispirited, they flung themselves down on the reeking plain of Isandhlwana, it is extremely likely that the general and every man with him would have been killed. The gross absurdity of blaming Lord Chelmsford for not burying the dead on the field is only equalled by its injustice. The general and the remnant of his column were really fugitives, and it was not until they found that, by the heroic defence of Rorke's Drift, the base of operations was still held, that they were able to breathe with any degree of safety. It was hoping against hope to imagine that a place really left unfortified could have been held against a victorious army; and it is well to recognize the fact that not only Natal and its people, but Lord Chelmsford and the remnant of his column, were saved by the heroes of this colonial Thermopylæ.

The awful pause of suspense, which lasted many weeks, passed by. The Tugela River and the indecision of the Zulu king saved the colony. Reinforcements which had been telegraphed for poured in with amazing celerity, and both Natal and British honour were saved. For nine weeks the beleaguered column under General Pearson had to suffer privations, and the Zulus, who had experienced what British soldiers could do behind biscuit-boxes at Rorke's Drift, hesitated to attack them when behind regular entrenchments at Ekowe. At last, as we had seen, relief was sent. Then another period of delay set in. Masses of troops continued to arrive, and early in May our strength in Natal comprised more than 23,000 men, divided as follows:—

First division (Gernrl Crealock's)	9,215
Second division (General Newdigate's)	10,238
General Wood's flying column	3,092
	———
Effective and non-effective	22,545

The following is a brief biography of the distinguished officer:—
General Henry Evelyn Wood, V.C, C.B., of the 90th Regiment, and commanding the column at Kambula, entered the Royal navy in 1852, and served in the Naval Brigade as A.D.C. to Captain Peel, of the *Shannon*, from 1st October, 1854, to 18th January, 1855, when he was severely wounded carrying up scal-

ing ladders to the Redan. He was mentioned in Lord Raglan's despatches (medal with clasps. Knight of the Legion of Honour, 5th Class of the Medjidie and Turkish medal). He next served in the Indian campaign of 1858 in the 17th Lancers, and as brigade-major in Somerset's Brigade, and was present at Rajghur, Sindwaho (mentioned in General Michel's despatches), Kharie, and Barode, mentioned in despatches (medal).

In 1859-60 he was employed, while commanding 1st Regiment Beatson's Horse, in hunting down rebels in the Seronge jungles; thanked by the Indian Government for his services, and received the Victoria Cross. He raised the 2nd Regiment Central Indian Horse. Accompanied Sir Garnet Wolseley to the Gold Coast in September, 1873, on special service, and served throughout the Ashantee war of 1873-4 Organized the natives forming "Wood's Regiment." Commanded the attacking force at the action of Essaman (received the expression of her Majesty's approbation).

Commanded the troops at the head of the road, following the enemy from Mansu to the River Piah, prior to the arrival of the European troops, including the reconnaissance in force of the 27th November. Commanded the right column at the battle of Amoaful (slightly wounded), and commanded the headquarters of his regiment at the battle of Ordahsu and capture of Coomassie (several times mentioned in despatches, brevet of colonel, C.B., medal with clasps). His Victoria Cross was gained for having, on the 19th of October, 1858, during action at Sandwaho, when in command of a troop of the 3rd Light Cavalry, attacked with much gallantry, almost single-handed, a body of rebels who had made a stand, whom he routed. Also, for having, subsequently, near Sindwaho, gallantly advanced with a *duffadar* and *sowar* of Beatson's Horse, and rescued from a band of robbers a *potail*, Chemmum Singh, whom they had captured and carried off to the jungles, where they intended to hang him.

This was a large army, the most powerful force of Europeans ever engaged in war within South Africa. The occasion was supreme, as the greatest power of the native races had challenged the white man to a combat *à l'outrance*, and the question simply was whether the Queen or Cetywayo should rule supreme in the southern portion of this continent. Reinforcements were sent out with immense celerity, and landed with the utmost despatch and with neither casualty nor danger. But the delay in moving them was most disappointing. It must have puzzled the Zulus immensely to understand why we were so extraordinarily slow. Five weeks had elapsed since the battle of Ginghelovo without any set engagement with the enemy taking place, and the Press began to grumble. Transport rose to unprecedented rates. Twenty shillings per cwt., or £20 per ton, was charged for the carriage of provisions a distance of fifty-four miles, from D'Urban to Pietermaritzburg.

Oxen died in hundreds, and the progress of the battalions of infantry which were marching against an enemy famous for their celerity was most disheartening. The plan of Lord Chelmsford was that of sending on masses of troops, whose *impedimenta* in the shape of baggage and means of supply was so enormous as to completely cripple their movements. At a subsequent period, after the arrival of Sir Garnet Wolseley, we shall find that officer successfully employing more than 2000 Zulu carriers; but this method, cheap and efficient, does not seem to have been tried by Lord Chelmsford.

To lessen the enormous difficulties of transport, which crushed the efforts of our soldiers, a successful attempt was made to find a landing-place on the Zululand coast. H.M. gunboat *Forester* was sent on this quest, which was ultimately successful, and Port Durnford was established as a place for landing supplies. This cut off more than a hundred miles of difficult road, and was of immense service to the advancing columns. During May, 1879, the *Forester*[1] performed important duties in this service, and more than once fired at bands of the enemy near the seashore.

It is impossible to write any chronicle of the movements of General Crealock's column which would be of interest. It crawled along among hundreds of dead oxen killed in dragging its heavy baggage and supplies over bad roads. Enormous expenditure for commissariat and transport services went on, and it was very evident that this war would be waged at frightful cost. The British lion growled in England, and there was an undoubted echo in the colonies.

On the 15th of May, the headquarters of the South African field force, under Major-General Newdigate, was situated on the Buffalo River, near Doornberg. The force comprised;—Right wing of the

---

1. Captain Bradshaw, of H.M.S. *Shah*, accompanied Captain Smith of the *Forester*. Mr. G. C. Cato, one of the oldest and most respected inhabitants of Natal, furnished important information with regard to a landing-place on the coast, and went in H.M.S. *Forester* to assist in choosing one.

17th Lancers; three companies 1-21st Regiment; six companies 58th; N battery, 5th Brigade, Royal Artillery, with six 7-pounders, raider Colonel Harness; N Battery, 6th Brigade, with six 9-pounders; Army Service Corps, Army Hospital Corps, Bengaugh's Native Battalion, Natal Pioneers, and Natal Carbineers. Colonel Tatton Browne commanded the Royal Artillery, and Captain Anstey the Royal Engineers.

Twelve miles further on, at Conference Hill, was the most advanced post, where Colonel Davies. Grenadier Guards, commanded. The garrison was composed of six companies of the 94th Regiment, Bettington's troop of Natal Horse, a detachment of the Royal Engineers, and Shepstone's Mounted Basutos. Another fort and *laager* had been erected for their defence, while eight miles further on towards the north-east was Brigadier-General Wood's new camp at Magwechana, close to the Sand Spruit, one of the sources of the White Umvolosi. General Marshall was with the cavalry camp.

The experience of Isandhlwana was thoroughly sufficient, and the most complete precautions on all occasions were taken to prevent the possibility of disaster. Forts and fortified positions covered the country, but, nevertheless, there is excellent authority for saying that if a Zulu *impi* had been ordered to invade, there would have been no difficulty in driving back the weak border guard which lined the Tugela, getting behind the regular forces, and making a rapid destructive raid and an equally rapid retreat.[2]

Cetywayo's neglect of his opportunities was more useful in protecting Natal than the immense armed force which, with infinite toil

---

2. A resident on the Tugela, writing to the *Natal Mercury* on the 7th of May, 1979, says, "It is my deliberate opinion that were the Zulus to cross the Tugela in force anywhere between Toohey's Drift and Fort Buckingham, they might avoid the military and make a raid into Natal easily. The general commanding has done all in his power to protect the border, by placing native guards, under white men, all along it; but their only use will be to give the alarm in case the Zulus attack. I have seen many of them, and I have asked them what they will do if the Zulus make an attack. 'Run, of course,' was the reply; and I have heard—not from them, but from at third person—that they have said, 'If our officers order us to cross the Tugela unsupported by white troops, we shall tell them to kill us in Natal, and save themselves the trouble of taking as to Zululand to be killed.' I therefore look upon the border guard as utterly worthless as a means of defence, and two at least of the volunteers at Thring's Post—intelligent men they are—entirely agree with me.

"What may be the state of affairs at Cetywayo's *kraal* I know not; bat this I do know, namely, that all along the Tugela border the Zulus have returned to and occupied their *kraals*, and that they sometimes shout defiance and exchange shots with the border guards."

and a slowness almost passing description, moved on towards Ulundi. Loud were the public outcries at the transport breakdown and the tardiness of operations. General Newdigate's magnificent force seemed paralyzed, and the difficulties of grass for horses and supplies for troops *en route* was the theme of every journal and the excuse for a delay which was as costly as it was disappointing.

On the 17th of May, a road was made in the direction of Landman's Drift, and a few days afterwards all the cavalry proceeded to Rorke's Drift, and thence to Isandhlwana, for the purpose of burying the dead. It was certainly full time to perform this duty. One of the disgraceful occurrences or sad consequences of the Zulu war is the fact, which cannot be slurred over without comment, that the bodies of our brave men who fell at Isandhlwana remained unburied for more than four months. Two regiments of Dragoon Guards, with the Lancers and numerous other troops, moved on with alacrity to perform the honourable task. The force advanced in line, *échelon*, or column of squadrons, with extensive advance and rear guards, as well as flankers.

At night the men bivouacked in groups of twelve, with their saddles turned inwards and placed in a circle. At last they looked down from the Biggarsberg upon Rorke's Drift and the Isandhlwana mountain in the distance. One regiment of the Lancers and one of the Dragoon Guards, as well as half the Natal Carbineers, swept the country in the neighbourhood. The smoke of blazing huts rose up like burnt-offerings from the hill-altars of Zululand. The signal-fires of the savages helped to light up the country at night, and the British were again on the field where Cetywayo had gained his first and last victory. General Marshall, with Dragoons, Lancers, irregular horse, police, and artillery, crossed the river at daybreak, and advanced in open order. But my readers will prefer to read an account of what was seen and done at Isandhlwana from the pen of a soldier who was there. The correspondent of the *Times* of Natal writes:—

> We pushed on very steadily and carefully, and at half-past nine our advance-guard was on the ridge overlooking the valley beyond Isandhlwana. There it lay, a magnificent stretch of country, with undulating plains for miles, only broken by dongas and email rises, and bordered by high hills on each side. Who would have thought, looking down on the quiet scene, that it had witnessed one of the most terrific fights and disasters of modern times? The grass had grown up over the whole site of what had once been our camp, and was thickly intermixed with *mealie*

stalks and oat hay, green and growing yet.

Among these lay the bodies of our poor soldiers, scattered about in all postures, and in all stages of decay; while the positions of our tents were indicated by the broken remains of boxes, trunks, tins of preserved meats, remnants of the tents themselves, and masses of disordered papers, books, and letters, etc., etc. The only thing, however, that at once drew the attention of a casual observer was the broken remains of wagons and the skeletons of horses and oxen. Everything else was hidden at first sight, and required searching for to be noticed. One thing we had observed coming along the road was the fresh spoor of a wagon or two, and we conjectured that it had been recently used in conveying crops from Sirayo's valley away into the strongholds further inland. The spoor of two mounted Kafirs, and one on foot, was also traced by the scouts fresh that morning; one of the horses was shod all round, and these men were evidently of the party left by the enemy to watch the coming of our troops.

For some time after our arrival, and while preparations were being actively carried out to harness the horses to the best wagons, all the men except those on *vedette* or other duty were allowed to wander over the scene of the disaster. The Carbineers, under Captain Shepstone, made immediately for their camp, and tried to find any relics of their dead brethren. Nothing of any consequence was, however, found near their lines; but upon searching over the ground where the bodies of some of them had been seen on the night after Isandhlwana, Captain Shepstone came upon the bodies of Colonel Durnford, Lieutenant Scott, and nearly all the Carbineers, except London and Bullock, and those few who were killed along the fugitive path.

Poor Durnford was easily recognisable, and he had on his mess waistcoat, from the pocket of which Shepstone took a small pocket-knife with his name on it. Two rings were also taken, and are with the knife to be sent home *in memoriam* to the colonel's father. Durrant Scott lay partially hidden under a broken piece of a wagon, and had evidently not been mutilated or touched after his death. He had his patrol jacket on, buttoned across, and although the rest of the body was only a skeleton, yet, strange to say, the face was like in life, all the hair being still on, and the skin strangely parched and dried up, although perfect.

Both these bodies lay right in the midst of the rest of the young colonists who fell gallantly in defence of their country; and, judging from the position in which they all were, they must have made one last gallant stand, and have been killed altogether. None of these so found had attempted to run, but had stuck together in life as we found them in death. Knowing all of them well, and how they did their duty, I felt it almost impossible to examine any, and had to leave the scene for another one. I can only add that Durnford's body was wrapped in canvas and buried in a kind of waterwash, while all the others were covered over with stones, etc., and their names written in pencil on wood or a stone close by them.

The bodies of the Royal Artillery and Natal Mounted Police were also buried, the only ones left untouched being those of the 24th Regiment, which was done at the express desire of Colonel Glyn and the officers, in the hope of their being able some day to do it themselves. This appeared, however, very strange to us, and many remarks were made about the seeming dishonour to part of our brave dead. However, let us hope that someday, not far distant, we may be able to return to that once blood-red field and bury all the bodies, bones, and relics that may be left. Great numbers of wagons have undoubtedly been taken away, as also everything of value in the camp, and many bodies have been, through one cause or another, either wholly or partially removed or disturbed, so as to effectually prevent recognition.

I myself did not move far out of camp, and, therefore, may be a bad judge, but from what I saw there cannot have been more than 200 bodies in the camp itself, and out of these not 25 Kafirs. Doubtless, had I gone out to where the fighting first commenced, I should have found many more bodies, but I am glad for my own sake that I did not do so. Others, who had not perhaps so many bitter feelings or sorrowful remembrances of those lying around us, went further and saw more, although I cannot hear of anyone having recognized any more bodies of officers, except those of the Hon. S. Vereker and young Gibson, both lieutenants in the Native Contingent. Many interesting relics were found and brought away by others, and I know of a few cases where letters addressed to relatives at home from those among the killed were found complete, and will be sent home, to be held in loving regard by the living, but will cause many sores scarce healed to be reopened.

The general was anxious, for more reasons than one, to get away, and therefore, as soon as the wagons were ready, we made a start back at twelve, and reached Rorke's Drift at half-past three without any hitch whatever. Immediately on getting back I went inquiring among the different parties who had been over that day, and gleaned some other interesting facts from them. One officer in the Dragoon Guards, while out with his squadron burning *kraals*, found in one signs of very recent occupation, and the staff of the Queen's colour of the 1-24th. He also later on came across a *kraal* full of skeletons of Zulus; and this fact, taken in conjunction with the finding of large graves on the left of our camp containing bodies of the enemy, goes far to prove that the Zulus did move their dead bodies, and as the *kraal* was some two miles off where skeletons were found, they probably also moved them in our wagons.

The forty wagons we brought away included two water carte in good preservation, one gun limber, a rocket battery cart, and three Scotch carts. All that we left behind, in number not more than twenty, were in a partially or entirely disabled condition. Counting all these, therefore, there are still sixty or seventy wagons missing, which have been taken away at different times.

The irregular horse recruited in the Cape Colony and Natal deserve special mention. Their services during the war were of a most important and valuable character. Most of them were attached to General Wood's column, and in the many daring raids in which their services were used proved excellent soldiers. Among the most prominent of these corps was that of the Kaffrarian Riflemen, under Commandant Schermbrucker. On the 30th of April, at Utrecht, on the occasion of the expiry of their engagement, that officer bade farewell to his officers and men in an eloquent address in which he recalled their principal services. Six months previously, on a public parade at Pietermaritzburg, they had been selected by Lord Chelmsford for a post of danger, in consequence of the manner in which they had fought on the borders of the Cape Colony during the Gaika rebellion.

For nearly three months the important and dangerous post of Luneberg had been held, and the handful of white men had indicted serious losses on the enemy, and secured safe communication *via* Intombe to Derby. They had been attached to "that glorious column" commanded by Evelyn Wood, and formed part of the forces under Buller engaged in the rescue of Oham's people at his surrender. They were also in the disastrous storming of the Zlobane and the glorious battle of Kambula. Admirable obedience and cheerful discipline were maintained in the face of 20,000 enemies.

Their last duties were the harassing ones of escorting convoys *en route* from Battle Spruit to Kambula.[3] What was said, and said truly, of Schermbrucker's Irregular Horse might be said with little variation of the other corps—Baker's, Whalley's, etc. Colonial men, such as Schermbrucker, Nettleton, Shepstone, Lonsdale, Blaine, Pickering, Wilson, and many others, distinguished themselves in the field, and it can be said with equal truth and justice that the volunteer force and levies, officers and men, proved most valuable auxiliaries.

The Transvaal Republic had dragged along a sad existence for many years, troubled constantly by native incursions from without, and debt, quarrelling, and discontent from within, when the Rev. Thomas F. Burgers was elected President in the year 1872. He was to revolutionize the entire country, and to make a new and improved Holland in Southern Africa. Gifted with certain talents, among which that of oratory was conspicuous, Burgers was deplorably deficient in a knowledge of men and business. His plans were utopian, visionary, and

---

3. A few particulars connected with the gallant Schermbrucker's movements cannot fail to be of interest. Having assumed command on April 15th, he directed his first attention to Luneberg, where he arrived with Colonel Bray, C.B., about the middle of May, when he reconnoitred in preparation for an attack upon Tafelberg (Umbellini's caves), accompanied by Captain Moore, 4th Regiment, and an orderly. They got too far within the enemy's lines, and with river and a dangerous *donga* between them, on the road back to camp found themselves attacked by about fifty Zulus, all armed with Martini-Henry rifles. The commandant was unarmed, except his British bull-dog (a little revolver). His horse was shot under him; Captain Moore's fell, also shot down dead. The orderly mounted behind the commandant was thrown again and again, whilst the Zulus came closer and closer. At last the orderly got somewhat confused and could not be remounted. He went down to the river to find a hole where he could eventually defend himself; Captain Moore then mounted behind the commandant, and after a fearful ride through the Zulus' bullets, which whistled about them like hailstones, they at last gained the camp, Without a minute's delay he started off with twenty mounted men to the relief of Larson (the name of the orderly). Alas! the poor fellow had disappeared. All searching was in vain, not the vestige of a spoor could be detected. On May 20th Tafelberg was attacked. One hundred Zulus in well-entrenched positions poured in a deadly fire. Lieutenant Gown, of the 4th Regiment, distinguished himself in a gallant charge, and the enemy were driven back into their caves and holes.—Extract from private letters.

unsound. He caused hundreds of Boers to leave their adopted country, by forcing on them a system of education from which the teachings of religion were excluded; contracted a loan of £300,000 for a railway from Delagoa Bay, which would have cost millions; designed a fanciful coat of arms and flag; caused gold coins to be issued with his own likeness stamped upon them, and played such "fantastic tricks before high heaven" as to help forward that crisis of bankruptcy and ruin from which it would have been very difficult, even by an exactly opposite course, to have saved the country.

During the absence of the President in Europe, in 1875, Sekukuni, the principal chief of the Bapedi people, broke out in rebellion. In April, 1876, he was called upon to submit, but in place of doing so boldly claimed the larger portion of the. Lydenburg and Pretoria districts. A commando then marched against him, and succeeded in taking "Mathebi's Kop," which was grandiloquently styled the Gibraltar of South Africa. A subsequent attack upon Sekukuni's head *kraal* was a failure. The prosecution of the war was then entrusted to volunteers, and after a short time an inglorious peace was concluded. This treaty was only made to be broken, as it was repudiated and treated with contempt by Sekokuni.

The peace of all British South Africa was seriously jeopardized by the weakness and fatuity of the Government of the Transvaal Republic. They were unable to conquer Sekukuni, and were so threatened by Cetywayo as to make an incursion by that potentate exceedingly probable. If the outworks of civilization were not looked after there would soon be serious danger to the fortress. Sir Theophilus Shepstone was therefore appointed special Commissioner. He arrived at Pretoria in January, 1877, and an extraordinary session of the Volksraad was held in February.

A radical reform, legislative, executive, and judicial, or the British flag, was the alternative laid before them. They chose the former, but remedies then came too late. The patient was incurable. President Burgers declared that a new constitution could not save them. On the 8th of March the *Raad* broke up, and on the 12th of April Sir Theophilaa Shepstone formally annexed the Transvaal territory to the British crown. It was, without doubt, incomparably the best course for a bankrupt country, perfectly unable to cope either with its debts or its foes, but it is very doubtful whether it was the wisest course for the British Government.

An immense burden was at once placed upon our shoulders, and the people furnished with a grievance easily fanned into discontent, and perhaps even into rebellion, by Hollanders and others who could make capital out of factious opposition and a trade out of revolution. If Sir Theophilus Shepstone had only waited long enough, the people would have begged upon their knees for protection and assistance when attacked by the enormous armies of the Zulu king. If we had intervened in such a crisis, we would have obtained the assistance—valuable assistance—of thousands of mounted burghers; whereas, when we did fight really for the Transvaal, its inhabitants were so disgusted with what had transpired, as to render almost no assistance.

There is no doubt that we managed the annexation of this country badly, and have been compelled to suffer for it. By a policy of delay, which would certainly have been less kind but incomparably more wise, the people would have been forced to come as suppliants for protection and annexation. Their lives and property when threatened by Cetywayo, could have alone been saved by British intervention. It can certainly be argued, on the other side, that delay was particularly dangerous, and that if we had not at once established ourselves In the Transvaal, the Zulus would have lighted a fire which would have spread quickly throughout every native tribe, and have endangered the peace of all our settlements. Sir Theophilus Shepstone was in an excellent position to judge of the necessity, and her Majesty's Government has uniformly upheld the policy adopted by him in annexing the Transvaal.

Sekukuni had proved a thorn in the side of the Republic which they had really been unable to get rid of. The peace with this chief was quite illusory, and only betrayed weakness on the part of the Dutch. We cannot be surprised, therefore, that he soon resumed hostilities. Under British rule an expedition was, in 1878, sent against him, consisting of volunteers and native police, under the command of Captain Clark. This force was not strong enough, and portions of the 13th and 80th Regiments, together with mounted infantry and volunteers, were despatched under Colonel Rowland. An unprecedented drought rendered operations almost impossible, and the expedition had to return, after leaving a portion of the 80th Regiment to guard the passes.

The great war with Cetywayo soon absorbed all our attention and efforts, therefore the attack on Sekukuni in his stronghold was postponed. It was reserved for Sir Garnet Wolseley to complete, late in 1879, that which had been commenced previous to the close of 1878. The rebellion of this native chief was specially one against the Republic of the Transvaal, and we had to take it over among the other heavy liabilities of that State.

Sir Bartle Frere found it desirable to proceed to Natal early in 1879, and remained there daring the crisis which resulted from the Isandhlwana disaster. On his return the High Commissioner passed through the Transvaal, and found that grumbling and discontent had been fomented into incipient rebellion. Mass meetings of the farmers were held, a people's committee was appointed, and a determination to recover their independence was freely expressed. With perfect firmness and straightforwardness, accompanied by admirable tact and patience, Sir Bartle Frere pointed out the real position of affairs.

Another petition to the Imperial Government for restoration of their independence was sent through the High Commissioner, and in this way the outbreak of feeling was calmed for the time. Special envoys had been previouslly sent in vain to gain this object, and it really seemed hoping against hope to imagine that the Imperial Government could again allow the re-establishment of such a republic as that which had been found unable either to defend or govern the people whom it was supposed to rule.

CHAPTER 8

Slow Operations

So far back as the 9th of February, Lord Chelmsford had written to the Home Government, requesting that an officer of the rank of major-general should be sent out at once. Sir Bartle Frere concurred in that representation, and suggested that the officer selected should be fitted to succeed him in the position of High Commissioner. On the 19th of March, the Secretary of State blamed Sir Bartle Frere for not having afforded her Majesty's Government an opportunity of considering the time as well as the manner of coming to issue—should it be necessary to come to issue—with the Zulu king. Sir Michael Hicks Beach says that this should have been done, although a favourable season for the operations of British troops might have been lost, and the means of further arming and victualling his forces given to Cetywayo; but the Secretary of State does not say, and of course could not say, that it should have been done at the imminent risk of the invasion and destruction of our colony at Natal.

Yet, after all, that is the true question. Sir Bartle Frere was specially charged, under his commission, with the protection of our own territory from native inroads, and was bound, in a great emergency, to make use of his immense delegated power in a prompt manner. Cetywayo, for two years, had been arranging for a great special blow upon the white people. He was crouching ready to spring, and the High Commissioner knew it was absolutely necessary to act at once.

The following information is from a colonist whose character and experience render him an unexceptionable witness. He says, "As a resident of many years in Zululand, I have had some experience and means of observation. The year before the Commission sat at Rorke's Drift, the chief Usirayo built his head *kraal* at Usogexe, and a strong stone wall with loopholes round it; and his people often told me that they hoped to use them against the white men. They often talked about war; and I more than once remonstrated with Usirayo and his people, telling them that they should take care not to bring about a war with '*abelungu*' (the white men), as it would be worse for themselves, but in vain, as they felt confident in their guns and their numbers. Cetywayo once sent an ox-hide to Sir T. Shepstone, and said, if he could count the hair on it, he would perhaps be able to form an idea of the number of the Zulu warriors; but I do not think the hide reached its destination.

When the Commission was sitting at Rorke's Drift, Usirayo threatened to destroy the men and tents, if they came across the Buffalo to inspect the border line, near Usirayo's head *kraal*, where you still see the stone heaps left since the beacons. I warned the Commission through a missionary, and the late Colonel Durnford noted it. The Zulus have bought their thousands of guns, for the purpose of using them against the whites; have bought most of their ammunition with the same intention; have engaged people from Basutoland to teach them to make powder; and they have had a good deal of training in shooting.

When Umbellini committed his first massacre at Umpongolo—I think in 1877—he went to the king, who adorned him with the usual sign of an '*iqawe*' (a plucky and brave fellow); so it seems to be little use in saying the king did not agree with the rascal in his doings, as somebody seems to mean. Why did the king allow Usirayo and his people to steal horses, cattle, and sheep from the Boers, year after year, without punishing them? Why did he not at once punish Usirayo and his men, for crossing the border with arms last winter, and dragging away the poor women, who had fled for their lives? Why has he tried to rouse other tribes against the whites? Why did be not care for the promises made at the coronation?

He wished for war, and he has got it; and that which brought him to that madness is chiefly this: First, that he despised the Gospel, of which he knows a good deal, and would not allow his people to become Christians; secondly, because the Christian Government would not allow him to make war upon other tribes, as his forefathers had done; and thirdly, his strong belief that he should succeed in exterminating the whites, because he thought them only a handful, and his own soldiers as plentiful as grass—which phrase be often uses with regard to them in conversation.

Could he but get rid of the whites, he would soon subdue the black tribes—that has been his hope. And now we must be thankful to God, who sent such a man as Sir Bartle Frere to save the colonists from such a blow as Cetywayo intended to have aimed at them.

Hence the commencement of hostilities early in January within Zululand. If there had been no disaster at Isandhlwana there would have been no censure. The ideas of Her Majesty's Government with regard to conditions of peace will be found expressed in the Secretary of State's despatch, dated the 20th of March:—No farther interference with the internal government is to be permitted than what is necessary for securing the peace and safety of the adjacent colonies. Duly authorised residents or agents to reside in the country. The Zulu military system to be discontinued, and missionaries to be admitted. These views necessarily subject to modification by future events.

The battle of Ghinghelovo was fought upon the 2nd of April, and the battle of Ulundi, which will be referred to in due course, took place on the 4th of July. A complete chronicle of the operations of the different columns during the interval would be most tiresome and uninteresting. Such a narrative would be occupied with little raids upon the enemy, and of the enemy upon us; occasional scares; the active operations from Wood's column in securing the country within forty miles; captures and losses of cattle; movement of troops; fort-building; camp life; and, above all, the troubles, anxieties, and annoyances of the slow march towards the front and the difficulties of transport. Messengers, ostensibly from the king, came in at various times to ask for peace; but, viewed in the light of subsequent events, there is little doubt that such people were merely sent as spies, with the double object of putting us off our guard and obtaining information. An engagement took place on the 5th of June, between the enemy and a portion of Brigadier-General Wood's column, which requires more than mere passing mention.

Paragraphs such as the following would frequently recur. A correspondent at the Lower Tugela writes, in May, "Knowing that the reinforcements have arrived, looking at and counting the forces now in the field, seeing the wagon road full of starving oxen which will very soon be unable to work, while the grass grows dry and scarce, and no sign is seen of the troops being ready to more, the talk in the papers of months being likely to pass before any operation can begin again, etc., really makes you sad and despairing, and causes you to fear that the whole Zulu war will be a failure. If any of the successes the English troops have had could have been followed up by speedy advances, the war would have been finished long ago; but as it is, it gives the enemy plenty of time to collect and reorganise, thinking that the English, checked by some unknown difficulties, most give it up at last altogether. If the campaign is to be directed from home it will be a failure, without doubt. Had the troops been able to advance a fortnight ago, we might now have seen something of the end of the war. This lingering cannot but have a bad effect upon the enemy, keeping up their hopes of an ultimate success.

Transport is now and more the bugbear. As we point out elsewhere, the simple fact it that the resources of the country are overstrained. Young and untrained cattle are, in many cases, being employed, at a very serious risk of loss. We are glad to learn, indirectly, that the proceedings of the commission of enquiry go to show that coat and difficulties of transport are at the bottom of the high charges complained of, and that the question is really one of supply and demand. The commissariat are now employing 1800 wagons, and want 200 more very urgently. There is, we believe, much exaggeration in the statements put forth as to the exorbitant charges made upon the commissariat. However, we await the report of the commission with much interest.

As an attack was expected on the line of march, reinforcements of cavalry (Lancers and Dragoons) as well as mounted natives were sent. Colonel Buller, with two troops of Frontier Light Horse, and detachments of Baker's and McDonald's forces, together with Cochrane's Mounted Basutos, formed a scouting force in advance. Lord William Beresford assisted Colonel Buller as staff officer. The 90th Regiment formed the advance-guard of the main column, the 80th was in the centre, and the 1-13th formed the rearguard. Two large bodies of Zulus, about 1000 in number, were observed near the large *kraal* of Usirayo, and they seemed by their position to challenge an attack.

Our men were ordered to advance at a trot, and the enemy retired into the belt of thornbush surrounding the base of the mountain, from which they poured a heavy fire. After half an hour's fusillade from each side the enemy's fire began to slacken. Lancers and Dragoons crossed the river, but, not being supported by artillery, were unable to dislodge the Zulus, and unfortunately lost Adjutant Frith, a young officer of great promise.

Subsequently the troop of Natal mounted natives under Shepstone checkmated an attempt of the enemy to cut off our retiring *vedettes*. After this the Zulus contented themselves with shouting out defiance. The British troops returned, having previously burned the *kraals* and ascertained the approximate number of the enemy assembled to oppose the march of the column. It is noteworthy that on this occasion the conduct of the regular troops and volunteers is described as manifesting both pluck and steadiness.[1]

We must now advert to the career of the most distinguished volunteer of the war, a prince who owned the most conspicuous dynastic name of the time—Napoleon Louis Bonaparte, Prince Imperial of France. Born in the purple and brought up amidst the greatest magnificence, the misfortunes of France became his own, and as an exile in England he studied at the Military College of Woolwich, where his success far surpassed even the sanguine expectations of his friends. The war in South Africa seemed to offer a sphere in which the heir of conquerors could learn to conquer. As a soldier, the prince earnestly desired to attain practical knowledge of his profession; as a Napoleon, he thirsted to distinguish himself by taking the sword each of his family had experienced to be the Key of Empire.

Great Britain was the refuge of his family, and among the soldiers of Great Britain he felt at home. On the 27th of February, 1879, Prince Louis Napoleon received the sacrament of the Catholic Church before the Emperor's tomb at Chiselhurst, and then embarked in the steamer *Danube* for the theatre of war. His determination to go to Zululand was absolutely his own act, and his brave mother had to yield to his judgment what her own heart opposed. The prince was singularly calculated to win the affection of all. Pure, wise, and Christian, he had declared, "If I am restored to the throne of my father, I will have none near me whose truth, honour, and morality are not above suspicion."

As free from affectation as possible, he was gay, simple, affable, and

---

1. Several correspondents of newspapers were under fire on this occasion, including those of the *Standard*, *Telegraph*, and *Daily Chronicle*.

so full of kindliness as to draw to him the hearts of all with whom he came in contact. On the voyage out he mixed with the passengers as one of them, joined in their games, and made himself beloved as much by the charm of his manner as the goodness of his nature.[2] Arrived at Cape Town, the prince became the guest of Lady Frere, the Governor being absent in Natal. He only remained there a few days, during the stay of the *Danube*, and went on in that steamer to Natal. The prince had received permission from the authorities to accompany the staff of the British army, and the Duke of Cambridge had written letters on this subject to Lord Chelmsford and to Sir Bartle Frere.

With that hatred of ostentation and desire of giving as little trouble as possible which markedly actuated all the proceedings of the prince, be merely took one servant to the front, and even left his faithful companion, M. Uhlmann, at D'Urban. Towards the end of April indisposition prevented his joining the headquarters staff of Lord Chelmsford, but he was delayed only a few days in Pietermaritzburg. It soon became evident to all his companions in arms that the prince was the bravest of the brave. No idea of fear ever crossed his mind, and as this undaunted disposition was not tempered by experience, it should have indeed greater watchfulness on the part of those men of high rank in the British army who were virtually his guardians during the campaign. In a reconnaissance which took place on Sunday, the 18th of May, the prince displayed that coolness in the face of danger for which he was remarkable.

On that day twenty-five men of Bettington's Horse, and the mounted Basutos under Colonel Harrison, accompanied by the Prince Imperial, crossed the Blood River, and subsequently descended into the Ityotyozi Valley, where they were to meet Colonel Buller and 300 men. They missed this force, however, and had to bivouac for the night near the south-east extremity of the Incqutu. No fires were allowed, and in shivering silence the night was passed, the enemy being expected at any moment. At daybreak they set off in quest of the road, and when approaching an ascent leading to a large *kraal*, were fired upon by sixty Zulus, who lined the ridge of rocks above.

---

2. At one at the Cape ports, a passenger remarked that a young man he noticed could not have been the prince, as he saw him at the foot of a ladder, handing into a boat the children of a poor workman. At Cape Town the crowd mistook a handsomely dressed young exquisite for the Prince Imperial, and were surprised when a simply dressed, unassuming youth stepped out of the steamer and entered the Governor's carriage, which was in waiting.

This fusillade was immediately returned, and without any hesitation Captain Bettington led straight up. The road was exceedingly steep and covered with boulders, but by a sudden charge the position was taken. Two Zulus were killed and seven horses captured. The prince evidently relished this engagement, and was as cool and collected throughout as if sitting in his study. In the captured *kraal* several relics of Isandhlwana were discovered, among which was a saddle of Colonel Black's, 2-24th, empty boxes of Martini-Henry, and an artillery forge bellows.

To show the narrow escapes which sometimes occurred, an incident that followed this little engagement may be related. Captain Bettington rode after three Zulus, two of whom were armed with guns and one with *assegai*. Thinking he was unarmed, they allowed him to come within ten yards. He called out and fired his revolver; two of the three loaded chambers missed fire, and one of the Zulus was just taking aim with his gun at a distance of only fifteen yards, when the third chamber exploded and the man fell dead. The other two ran away, and the remainder of the patrol came up shortly afterwards.

The prince was exceedingly fond of real work, and of sharing every privation and danger of his comrades. He was no feather-bed soldier. Anxious always to go out with patrols and on reconnaissance duty, it would have seemed ungracious to check his ardour, but his own daring and utter absence of fear made it specially necessary that men of tried experience should accompany him. At the commencement of June the Prince Imperial, attached to the Quartermaster-General's department, was at General Newdigate's camp. He had applied for and obtained leave to go on ahead of the division to the site of the new camp about to be formed. On the morning of the 1st of June, the reconnoitring party set out, consisting of the Prince Imperial, Lieutenant Carey of H.M. 98th Regiment, six selected men of Bettington's Horse, and one Kafir.

Six mounted Basutos had been ordered to join the party, but they were left behind. The spot to which they were about to proceed was familiar to the prince, and he was aware that it was in the vicinity of Lord Chelmsford's camp on one side, and of General Wood's on the other. The party started at half-past nine o'clock, and when they arrived at the neck of the Incenci Mountain were joined by some officers, who, after riding some distance with them, went off towards the left, in the direction of General Wood's camp. After crossing a rivulet which forms a tributary to the Ityotyozi River, they reached a large flat-topped hill, and there the prince, ordering the men to slacken girths for a little, took a sketch of the country.[3]

Shortly after the march was resumed, the prince pointed out the *kraal* from which he had been fired upon on a previous occasion, and turned off to examine another one, which was found empty. Immediately afterwards the party descended towards a third *kraal*, about a mile further on, as the prince observed a small river—the Mbazani—at which the horses could be watered, and where coffee could be made for the men. The *kraal* consisted of five huts, with a small stone enclosure, and was distant about 200 yards from the river. In front there was an open space, on which fires for cooking had been made, but between the *kraal* and the river *tambookie* grass grew, five or six feet in height, with *mealies* and Kafir corn interspersed. The party halted on the open space, and the prince gave the order to "off saddle" for an hour. No sign of life was visible, except where two or three dogs furtively ran from the intruders. Water was obtained, coffee made, the horses were turned into the grass and grain crops, while with a feeling of perfect security all lay stretched, resting, on the ground.

The hour quickly passed, and daring that time, unknown and unsuspected, fifty Zulus crawled in ambush preparing to make a spring. The position of the ground was most advantageous for their purpose. A deep *donga* formed excellent cover, and out of that they crept along the water's edge, completely screened by the rank vegetation. It was while they were thus concealed that one of them was seen by the Kafir sent to bring water to the Prince Imperial's party. The Zulu burst out of his ambush and fled. The Kafir returned and reported what he had seen. Meanwhile the prince, looking at his watch, remarked, "You can give your horses ten minutes more." What the Kafir reported had, however, made every one anxious to go, and the horses were caught and saddled.

All stood ready, and the prince examined the bit of his horse for a few moments. Then came the words, "Prepare to mount! Mount!" and almost at the same moment a volley fired from forty rifles, at a distance of twenty yards, crashed among them. At this time the party were standing in line, close to their horses, with their backs to the *kraal* and their faces tamed eastward, the prince being in front and nearest to the Zulus. Then with a tremendous cry, "*Usutu!*" and "Lo, the English cowards!" the savages rushed on. The horses immediately swerved,

3. The prince had already become noted for skill in sketching, and for remarkable ability in recognizing the capabilities of positions.

and some broke away.

An undoubted panic seized the party; everyone who could spring on his horse mounted and galloped for his life. There was no thought nor idea of standing fast and resisting this sudden attack. The prince was unwounded, but unable to mount his charger, which was sixteen hands high, and always difficult to mount. On this occasion the horse became so frightened by the firing and sudden stampede, as to rear and prance in such a manner as to make it impossible for the prince to gain the saddle. Many of the others saw the difficulty, but none waited or tried to give the least assistance. One by one they rushed their horses past. Private Le Tocq exclaiming as he went by, lying across his saddle, "*Dépêchez-vous, s'il vous plaêt, monsieur.*"

The prince, making no reply, strained every nerve, but, alas! in vain, to gain the back of his horse, holding his stirrup-leather with his left hand and the saddle with his right. With the help of the holster he made one desperate effort, but the holster partially gave way, and it must have been then that the horse trod upon him, and galled off, leaving his master prostrate on the ground. The prince then regained his feet and ran after his friends, who were far in advance. Twelve or thirteen Zulus were at this time only a few feet behind him. The prince then turned round, and, sword in hand, faced his pursuers. From the first he had never called for help, and now died bravely with his face to the foes, fighting courageously to the last. It is thought that the Zulus hurled their *assegais* at him, and that he quickly fell dead, pierced through the eye by a mortal wound.

In death, as in life, the Prince Imperial of France behaved as a brave soldier, the worthy heir of a great cause and a true son of France. No torture or pain accompanied his last moments. His first wound was mortal, and the noble and beloved prince in his last moments, as during his entire career, did nothing to sully the name he bore or the country which gave him birth.

Two of the troopers were shot. One of them, Rogers, never reached his horse, and received his death wound when standing by a hut, rifle in hand, preparing to defend himself. Trooper Abel was shot at the first discharge—at all events, before he could reach the *donga*. The kafir who had accompanied them and had brought the water for coffee, was quickly surrounded and killed. The rest of the party galloped off at full speed. Lieutenant Carey and two others crossed the donga at a difficult place, while the others, who were followed by the prince, took an easier route. The direction taken by the fugitives was General

Wood's camp.

Lieutenant Carey, shortly after starting, called out, "Keep to the left, and cross the *donga*, and rally behind it." At the same time he noticed Zulus apparently endeavouring to cut off their retreat. On a rise a little further on, he looked round, and one of the troopers, who happened to be near him, called attention to the prince's horse galloping away. In reply to a question, the man said it was useless to return. The other troopers were then 200 yards distant. Lieutenant Carey shouted out to them to keep to the left, and all made the best of their way to the camp, which was reached at 6.30 p.m.

It ought specially to be noted that the attack of the Zulus was a thorough surprise by an overwhelming force. No sentries had been posted, nor precautions of any kind taken, and at the time of the attack no carbines were loaded. Lieutenant Carey says that he did not notice the prince after he saw him mounting, and that he did not perceive any fighting when he looked round.

General Wood and Colonel Buller met Lieutenant Carey and the other survivors of the party. These officers were at the time about six miles from camp, and four or five from Isandhlwana mountain, when they saw five white men riding as if for their lives under the hills on the right. So soon as the fugitives saw the general and his escort, they came up to them at full gallop, and told the dreadful news. By means of field-glasses three horses were seen being led off at a distance of about seven miles, accompanied by twenty or thirty Zulus on foot. It was then nearly five in the afternoon, and too late to do anything.

On the following morning (Whit Monday) the advanced guard of Natal Native Contingent and Raaff's Horse pushed forward from Wood's camp to the scene of the disaster. They were joined there by squadrons of Lancers and Dragoons from General Newdigate. The search for the bodies was not a long one. That of poor Rogers was first found, lying stark naked, riddled with *assegai* stabs and with a gash in the abdomen. Thirty yards distant was that of Abel in the same condition. A wound in his right hand seemed to show that he had fought for his life at close quarters. Thirty yards or so from this, and in the *donga*, lay the corpse of the Prince Imperial.

Surgeon-Major Scott, specially deputed for the purpose by Lord Chelmsford, took charge of the body and proceeded to examine it. There was one longish wound on the right breast, which was evidently mortal; an *assegai* had pierced the right eye, and had at once either caused death or paralysis to pain. There were two wounds in the left side, and less serious ones all over the upper part of the chest. A long gash in the abdomen exposed the intestines, but had not injured them. Round the neck was a small gold chain, to which was attached a medal and Agnus Dei. These the Zulus had not dared to touch, as they look upon all such articles as charms to be dreaded. The body of the prince was then conveyed to camp, and those of the troopers were buried with religious ceremony.

It is now necessary to furnish the evidence taken at the court-martial and the statement of Lieutenant Carey. The preliminary report was as follows:—

> The Court is of opinion that Lieutenant Carey did not understand the position in which he stood towards the prince, and, as a consequence, failed to estimate aright the responsibility which fell to his lot. Colonel Harrison states that the senior combatant officer. Lieutenant Carey, D.A.Q.M.G., was, as a matter of course, in charge of the party, whilst on the other hand Carey says, when alluding to the escort, 'I did not consider I had any authority over it, after the precise and careful instructions of Lord Chelmsford as to the position the prince held.' As to his being invariably accompanied by an escort in charge of an officer, the Court considers that the possibility of such a difference of opinion should not have existed between two officers of the same department.
>
> The Court is of opinion that Carey is much to blame for having proceeded on the duty in question with a portion only of the escort detailed by Colonel Harrison. The Court cannot admit the irresponsibility for this on the part of Carey, inasmuch as he took steps to obtain the escort, and failed in so doing. Moreover, the fact that Harrison was present upon the Itelezi range gave him the opportunity of consulting him on the matter, of which he failed to avail himself. The Court, having examined the ground, is of opinion that the selection of the *kraal* where a halt was made and the horses off saddled, surrounded as it was by cover for an enemy, and adjacent to difficult ground, showed a lamentable want of military prudence. The Court deeply regrets that no effort was made after the attack to rally the escort, and to show a front to the enemy, whereby the possibility of aiding those who had failed to make good their retreat might have been ascertained.—Signed by General Marshall; Colonel Malthus, 94th Regiment'; Major Le Grice, RA.

On this report a court-martial was summoned by Lord Chelmsford, for the trial Lieutenant Carey, for having misbehaved before the enemy on the 1st June, 1879, when in command of an escort in attendance on the prince, who was making reconnaissances in Zululand, in having, when the prince and escort were attacked by the enemy, galloped away, and in not having attempted to rally them or otherwise defend the prince. The Court, under the presidency of Colonel Glyn, consisted of Colonels Whitehead, Courtney, Harness, Major Bouverie, and Major Anstruther.

Judge-Advocate Brander prosecuted, and Captain Crookenden, R.A., was for the defence.

When the Court opened the plan of the ground was proved.

Corporal Grubb and the prince gave the order "Off saddle" at the *kraal*, and "Prepare to mount." The prince mounted. After the volley, he saw Carey putting spurs to his horse, and he did the same. He saw Abel fall, and Rogers trying to get a shot at the Zulus. Le Tocq passed him, and said, "Put spurs to your horse, boy; the prince is down! "He looked round and saw the prince under his horse. A short time after the prince's horse came up, and he (Grubb) caught it. No orders were given to rally.

Le Tocq was called, and said: The prince told the natives to search the kraals, and finding no one there they off saddled. At the volley, he mounted, but, dropping his carbine, stopped to pick it up. In remounting he could not get his leg over the saddle. He passed the prince, and said in French, "Hasten to mount your horse," The prince did not answer. He saw the prince's horse treading on his leg. The prince was in command of the party. He believed Carey and the prince would have passed on different sides of a hut in fast flight, and it was possible that Carey might have failed to see that the prince was in difficulty. It was 250 yards from where he saw the prince down to the spot where he died.

Trooper Cochrane was called, and said: The prince was not in the saddle at the time of mounting. He saw, about fifty yards off, the prince running down the *donga* with fourteen Zulus in close pursuit. Nothing was done to help him. He heard no orders given, and did not tell Carey what he had seen until sometime after. He was an old soldier. He did not think any rally could have been made.

The Court then adjourned to the next day. On reassembling, the first witness called was—Sergeant Willis, who stated that he had seen Trooper Rogers lying on the ground by the side of his horse, close to the *kraal*, as he left the spot. He thought he saw the prince wounded at the same time that Trooper Abel threw up his arms. He thought the prince might have been dragged to the place where he was found after death, and that a rally might have been made twenty yards beyond the donga.

Colonel Harrison being called, stated that Carey was senior combatant officer, and must therefore have been in command of the party. Carey volunteered to go on the reconnaissance to verify certain points of his sketch. The prince was ordered to go to report more fully on the ground. He had given the prince into Carey's charge.

Examined by the Court, Colonel Harrison stated that when the prince was attached to his department he was not told to treat him as a royal personage in the matter of escort, but as any other officer, taking due precaution against any possible danger.

Dr. Scott (the prince's medical attendant) was then called, and stated that the prince was killed by eighteen *assegai* wounds, any five of which would have been fatal. There were no bullet wounds. The prince died where the body was found.

This closed the case for the prosecution. The defence called again—

Colonel Harrison, who testified to Carey's abilities as a staff officer, and said he had every confidence in him.

Colonel Bellairs was also called, and stated that it was in consequence of the occurrence of the 1st June that Carey had been deposed from his staff appointment the day previous to his trial.

Lieutenant Carey here submitted that his case had been prejudged, and that he had been punished before his trial.

The following is Lieutenant Carey's statement:—

On the 31st May, I was informed by Colonel Harrison, A.Q.M.G., that the Prince Imperial was to start on the 1st June, to ride over the road selected by me for the advance of the column, for the purpose of selecting a camping ground for the 2nd June. I suggested at once that I should be allowed to go with him, as I knew the road and wanted to go over it again for the purpose of verifying certain points. To this Colonel Harrison consented, reminding me that the prince was going at his own request to do this work, and that I was not to interfere with him in any way.

For our escort, six Europeans of Bettington's Horse and six Basutos were ordered. Bettington's men were paraded at 9 a.m., but owing to some misunderstanding the Basutos did not turn up, and, the prince being desirous of proceeding at, once, we went without them. On arriving at the ridge between Itelezi and Incenci, I suggested waiting for them, but the prince replied, 'Oh no; we are quite strong enough,' or words to that effect.

We proceeded on our reconnaissance from there, halting about half an hour on a high hill overlooking the Ityotyozi for the prince to sketch. From here the country was visible for miles, and no sign of the enemy could be discovered. We then descended into the valley, and, entering a *kraal*, off saddled, knee-haltering our horses. We had seen the deserted appearance of the country, and, though the *kraal* was to the right surrounded by *mealies*, we thought there was no danger in encamping.

If any blame is attributable to anyone for this, it is to me, as I agreed with the prince that we were perfectly safe. I had been over this ground twice before, and seen no one, and the brigade-major of the cavalry brigade had ridden over it with only two or three men, and laughed at me for taking so large an escort. We had with us a friendly Zulu, who, in answer to my inquiries, said no Zulus were about. I trusted in him, but still kept a sharp lookout, telescope in hand.

In about an hour—that is, at 3.40 p.m.—the prince ordered us to saddle up. We went into the *mealies* to catch our horses, but took at least ten minutes saddling. While doing so, the Zulu guide informed us he had seen a Zulu in the distance, but as he did not appear concerned, I saw no danger. The prince was saddled up first, and, seeing him ready, I mounted, the men not being quite ready. The prince then asked if they were all ready; they answered in the affirmative, and he gave the word 'Prepare to mount.'

At this moment I turned round, and saw the prince with his foot in the stirrup, looking at the men. Presently I heard him say, 'Mount,' and turning to the men, saw them vault into their saddles. At this moment my eyes fell on about twenty black faces in the *mealies*, twenty to thirty yards off, and I saw puffs of smoke and beard a rattling volley, followed by a rush, with shouts of '*Usutu!*' There was at once a stampede. Two men rushed past me, and as everyone appeared to be mounted, I dug the spurs into my horse, which had already started of his own accord. I felt sure no one was wounded by the volley, as I heard no cry, and I shouted out, 'Keep to the left, and cross the *donga*, and rally behind it!'

At the same time I saw more Zulus in the *mealies* on our left flank, cutting off our retreat. I crossed the *donga* behind two or three men, but could only get beyond one man, the others having ridden off. Riding a few hundred yards on to the rise, I stopped and looked round. I could see the Zulus after us, and saw that the men were escaping to the right, and that no one appeared on the other side of the *donga*. The man beside me then drew my attention to the prince's horse, which was galloping away on the other side of the *donga*, saying, 'I fear the prince is killed, sir.'

I immediately said, 'Do you think it is any use going back?' The trooper pointed to the *mealies* on our left, which appeared full of Kafirs, and said, 'He is dead long ago, sir: they *assegai* wounded men at once.' I considered he had fallen near the *kraal*, as his horse was going from that direction, and it was useless to sacrifice more lives. I had but one man near me, the others being some 200 yards down the valley.

I accordingly shouted to them to close to the left, and rode on to gain a drift over the Tombokala River, saying to the man at my side, 'We will keep back towards General Wood's camp, not returning the same way we came, and then come back with some Dragoons to get the bodies.' We reached camp about 6.30 p.m. When we were attacked our carbines were unloaded, and, to the best of my belief, no shots were fired.

I did not see the prince after I saw him mounting, but he was mounted on a swift horse, and I thought he was close to me. Besides the prince, we lost two troopers, as well as the friendly Zulu. Two troopers have been found between the *donga* and the *kraal*, covered with *assegai* wounds. They must have fallen in the retreat and been *assegaied* at once, as I saw no fighting when I looked round.

A shudder of horror and reproachful regret passed through Natal. It was sorrowful that the prince should be killed, but doubly lamentable that he should fall by the *assegais* of savages when his comrades deserted him. In the army the feeling of indignation and regret was particularly strong; and, however desirous men felt to do justice, it was scarcely possible for human nature to be entirely free from prejudice in forming a judgment with regard to the conduct of those who had been with the prince on the fatal day of his death. The court-martial condemned Lieutenant Carey, and sent him home under arrest. But a reaction of opinion subsequently took place. The Empress interceded for the unfortunate man, and our own Queen was pleased to order his release from arrest.

The death of the Prince Imperial was felt as a personal grief by every colonist. It spread gloom throughout the country, and recalled rigidly the shock that followed the disaster at Isandhlwana. The generous ardour with which the prince had given his services to the cause of the colonists seemed to have received a pitiful return. The heir of an Empire was dead, and the news must go hence to a widowed mother, who had made England her home. Every possible manifestation of grief and respect was paid. The military and the military authorities vied with the civil authorities and the people in doing honour to the illustrious dead. Natal went into mourning.

When the corpse arrived at Pietermaritzburg, people of all classes crowded into the streets to show their respect by joining the procession. The *Times* of Natal tells us that on the 8th of June, at 1.15 p.m., a gun was fired from Fort Napier, announcing that the body had arrived within two miles of the city, and by two o'clock a number which must have exceeded 3000 had assembled at the place of rendezvous on the Commercial Road. Here the procession was formed, the military headed by Major-General the Hon. H. H. Clifford, Inspector-General of Communications, on the one side; and the civilians, headed by his Excellency Sir Henry Bulwer, the Lieutenant-Governor of the colony, on the other.

Thousands of people lined the way up to the place where the procession had to fall in, and some time was taken before all were in their places in the order above indicated. Following the civil authorities, came the City Guard, some sixty strong, under Colonel Mitchell as general leader, and J. H. Spence as district leader; and after them came a large number of the Odd Fellows and Foresters in the funeral insignia of their order. After this the general public followed, all in mourning.

The arrangements being completed, amid the solemn booming of the minute guns, and the tolling of the church bells, the gun-carriage bearing the coffin was seen slowly coming down the hill, accompanied by the escort of regulars and mounted police which had come with it. As it approached the military fell into their places, and there was a hush which spoke, more eloquently than any words, the feelings of the vast concourse of people as the body of the late prince approached.

As the *cortége* passed every hat was raised in respect, and the military presented arms. The coffin was wrapped in a large tricolour, and upon it was a helmet and sword, together with wreaths of roses and camellias, and a beautiful cross of violets; while the grey charger, draped with a black pall, with the letter "N" on the corners, and with the boots reversed, according to military custom, followed. The procession then formed in the order given above, Major-General Clifford and the Lieutenant-Governor being immediately in front, while behind it were Fathers De Lacy and Baudry, the latter of whom had just come down with the body.

In the procession were observed many clergy of the English Church and of other denominations, among them the Right Reverend Bishop Colenso, the Right Reverend Bishop Macrorie, Dean Green, Archdeacon Ushervood, the Rev. Q. M. St. M. Ritchie, chaplain to the forces, etc., etc. The two valets of the late prince immediately followed the Catholic clergy. The pall-bearers were Captain Willoughby, 21st Scots Fusiliers; Captain Fox, R.A., D.A.A.G.; Major Russell, 12th Lancers; Lieutenant-Colonel East, 57th Foot, D.Q.M.G.; Lieutenant-Colonel Steward, R.E.; Colonel Reilly, C.B., R.H.A. The personal staff in attendance upon Major-General Clifford were Captain Fox, R.A., D.A.A.G., and Lieutenant Westmacott, 77th Regiment, A.D.C. General Bisset was also present, in full uniform. Major Spalding, D.A.A.G., acted as adjutant-general, in the absence of Colonel Bellairs. Amongst the civil servants were the Attorney-General, Hon. M. H. Gallwey; the Colonial Treasurer, Hon. Mr. Polkinghorne; the Surveyor-General, Mr. F. C. Sutherland, M.D.; the Mayor of Maritzburg, Mr. W. Francis, and the Town Councillors; Mr. W. Akerman, M.L.C., and Mr. C. C. Griffin, M.L.C.; and all the heads of departments who were not either absent from Maritzburg or prevented from being present by sickness.

The Maritzburg Rifles assembled in full number, under Lieutenant and Adjutant Scoones, and their band played the Dead March in "Saul," adding greatly to the solemnity of the procession. It marched slowly up Commercial Road to the corner of Church Street, up which it turned, and then wheeled along Chapel Street into Longmarket Street, arriving at the Roman Catholic School at about ten minutes before four. Here the coffin was taken from the gun-carriage by the pall-bearers, and conveyed into the chapel, followed by as many of the procession as the building would hold, the military who were on the ground being formed into two lines outside the building.

The Rev. Father Barrett met the procession at the door, and, together with Father De Lacy and Father Baudry, officiated, reading a short service over the coffin; all present appearing deeply affected. The military were then drawn up outside the building, and his Excellency and other distinguished personages passed through the lines, and the doors of the building were then closed upon the mortal remains of the late lamented prince.

The following special order had been issued by General Clifford:—

Wednesday, June 4th.

The Inspector-General of Lines of Communication and Base has received from his Excellency the Lieutenant- General commanding official confirmation of the calamity which has befallen the forces under his command, by the death, on duty in the field, of the late gallant young soldier the Prince Imperial, Louis Napoleon, who, having in his military training been associated with the British army, came out to this country to take part in the Zulu campaign.

The Inspector-General feels that he is carrying out the wishes of his Excellency the Lieutenant-General commanding, now in Zululand, by thus recording the feelings of deep sorrow and sympathy, experienced by every officer and man whose duty keeps him at his post in the colony, with the loss thus sustained.

The body of the unfortunate prince will arrive here probably on Monday next, the 9th inst., *en route* to England. Arrangements will be made to receive it with all due respect and expression of sorrow.

From the capital city of Pietermaritzburg, the body of the prince was conveyed to D'Urban, the seaport, and at the latter place the following eloquent special order was issued by the Assistant Adjutant-General.[4]

10th June, 1879.

The mortal remains of Prince Louis Napoleon will be carried tomorrow, at half-past 9 a.m., from the Roman Catholic Church, in D'Urban, to the Wharf, at Port Natal, for embarka-

---

4. Major W. F. Butler, author of *The Great Lone Land*.

tion in H.M.S. *Boadicea* to England.

In following the coffin which holds the body of the late Prince Imperial of France, and paying to his ashes the final tribute of sorrow and of honour, the troops in garrison will remember:—

First. That he was the last inheritor of a mighty name, and of a great military renown.

Second. That he was the son of England's firm ally in dangerous days.

Third. That he was the sole child of a widowed Empress, who is now left throneless and childless, in exile, on English shores.

Deepening the profound sorrow, and the solemn reverence that attaches to these memories, the troops will also remember that the Prince Imperial of France fell fighting as a British soldier.

W. P. Butler,

A.A.-General, Base of Operations.

D'Urban, Natal, South Africa.

The Roman Catholic Church at D'Urban was transformed into a *chapelle ardente*, and the coffin remained there all night after its arrival. Solemn requiem Mass was celebrated the next morning. The *Natal Mercury* tells us that by nine o'clock an immense crowd of persons had assembled outside the church where the gun-carriage was in waiting, and every arrangement had been made for speedily forming the procession after the ceremony was over. The principal object of interest outside was the grey horse belonging to the late prince, which he had purchased from a D'Urban gentleman, and the groom in charge of it was busily engaged in answering questions put to him with regard to the late prince. The horse was saddled, and in just the same condition as it was when it came back riderless to the camp.

The troops outside waiting to take part in the procession numbered altogether 700; the whole, as on the previous day, being under the command of Major Huskisson, commandant of the garrison. Every regiment doing service in South Africa was represented, including even the Dragoons and Lancers. At a quarter to ten the doors of the church were thrown open, and the coffin was brought to the gun-carriage, the honour of carrying it having been conferred on Captain Haynes (staff paymaster), Captain Granville (commissariat), Captain Young (commissariat), Captain Brunker, Commissary Marsh (ordnance), and Surgeon-Major Leslie. The procession was constituted as follows:—

	The band.	
Guard of honour. Pall bearers.	The body.	**Guard of honour. Pall bearers.**
	Chief mourners.	
	Military.	
Military and Volunteers.	Friendly societies.	**Civilians four-deep.**
	Public bodies.	
	Town guard.	
	Consular officers.	
	Heads of departments.	
	Archdeacon and clergy.	
	Members executive and legislative.	
	Mayor and Town Council.	
	Public schools.	
	The public.	

Having proceeded to the Point, the coffin was conveyed by a small steamer to H.M.S. *Boadicea*, where it was taken on board and hoisted into the hold of the vessel amid all the reverent marks of respect so fitting for the occasion. Monsieur Deleage, correspondent of the Paris *Figaro*, with two of the prince's attendants, accompanied the remains.

We will conclude this sad chapter of the history of the Zulu war by inserting a copy of the address signed in Natal, expressing deep sympathy with the widowed Empress:—

A Sa Majesté l'Imperatrice Eugénie.

Madame,

Les sous-signés, habitants de Natal, viennent respectueusement ex-primer à votre Majesté Impériale leurs sentiments de douloureuse sympathie, à l'occasion de la mort du jeune et vaillant prince votre fils, tombé à la fleur de l'âge, victime de ses sentiments de dévouement à une noble cause.

En présence d'one telle infortune qui cause taut de regrets et emporte de si brillantes espérances à votre cœur de mère, dejà si éprouvé, tous les colons de Natal, sont emus d'un même et unique sentiment de profonde affliction dont cette respectueuse adresse, n'est que la faible

Nous prions Dieu, Madame, de vouloir bien répandre sur votre Majesté les consolations que lui seul peut donner. En effet, votre douleur est si

grande, qu'il semble impossible à notre nature d'en supporter le poide.
Nous avons l'honneur d'être, avec le plus profond respect.

de votre Majesté Impériale,
Les très humbles et obéissants serviteurs.

CHAPTER 9

Battle of Ulundi

The policy of Sir Bartle Frere received the hearty and most earnest support of those people who were best qualified to judge of it, the colonists of Natal and the Cape Colony. At large and enthusiastic public meetings held in every town of any consequence unanimous votes of approval and sympathy were passed. In the city of Cape Town a great mass meeting declared unanimously for Sir Bartle Frere. Graham's Town expressed itself in the same manner. Fort Elizabeth notified its fullest confidence in his Excellency the High Commissioner, "being persuaded that the policy he is seeking to carry out in South Africa is eminently calculated to secure the permanent tranquillity of the country and the welfare of its inhabitants. King William's Town heartily sympathizes with his Excellency, and expresses its entire confidence." Graaff-Beinet, "having heard with the greatest satisfaction the manner in which the metropolis has come forward to approve of the policy of his Excellency Sir Bartle Frere, cordially endorses the Cape Town resolution." Swellendam recorded its "satisfaction with the well-timed movement in Cape Town;" George Town notified its approval; Queen's Town expressed its cordial sympathy and confidence; Kimberley declared strongly in favour of Sir Bartle Frere, and, of course, so did Pietermaritzburg, D'Urban, and other towns in Natal.

In fact, from east to west, from north to south, all classes, all creeds, all nationalities, were unanimous in upholding the only policy which they considered could serve South Africa. Bishop Colenso in Natal, and several other able men in Cape Town, held different views, but then their number was so very small as to detract in a very small measure from the unanimity of the expression of feeling. At these public meetings hearty votes of thanks were also passed to her Majesty's Government for having sent out reinforcements. There can be no doubt whatever that during April, May, and June, there was a very dissatisfied feeling in the colonies, as well as at home, with regard to the exceeding tardiness of operations. The small irritating raids made at different times upon Zululand cannot be styled successful, and resulted in reprisals which were calculated to have a demoralizing effect upon our own natives.

If Colonel Wood had been reasonably reinforced and allowed to go forward, there is good reason to believe that he could have finished the war. Up to the 18th of May his troops had been successful in seven skirmishes and one pitched battle. They had burnt the great Maquilizine military *kraal*, and captured 9000 head of cattle. This light brigade was admirably adapted for Zulu warfare. Pearson's column on the coast had also performed admirable service. The extraordinary difficulties and delays of transport under the new organization in the second campaign have been already referred to.

Lord Chelmsford, writing to the Secretary of State from Newcastle, Natal, on the 14th of May, states that the troops are in position, only waiting for sufficient supplies and transport to advance. From what the general commanding had learnt from General Clifford,[1] he feared that it would be out of his power to advance until the 1st of June. Major-General Crealock, commanding the first (coast) division, reported that he hoped to have two months' supplies in three weeks' time on the Inyezane river. The poets on the northern line had all been visited, and headquarters fixed at Utrecht, until such time as the second division, under General Newdigate, was ready to advance. Shortly afterwards, information was received that the border tribes were massing at Babincinqu and Inyayene, two points near the Blood River, and that the Zulus had sent for reinforcements to Ulundi.

Rest and security for two entire months had now been given to the enemy, and their determination to continue the war was perfectly evident, in spite of the illusory messages, asking for conditions of peace, which were periodically sent to the British camps. On the 26th of May, General Wood advanced his column eight miles, and General Newdigate proceeded a distance of twelve miles towards the Blood River. Lord Chelmsford established his headquarters at Kopje Alleen. Not until the middle of June could Port Dornford be used for sending supplies to General Crealock's coast column. Great additional transport facilities were by this means secured.

---

1. General Clifford remained in Pietermaritzburg; and was charged with the defence of Natal.

On June 3rd a belief prevailed at the Lower Tugela that an advance would be made as soon as the supply of cattle for transport purposes was sufficient. During all the operations the percentage of sickness was not very great. In the early part of the war a large number of men were invalided, particularly from the coast column. The D'Urban hospitals were full, but the number of deaths was not large, and as the cold season advanced sickness became less. Zululand, during May, June, and July, is, in fact, as healthy as any country in the world.

The two northern columns moved on slowly. On the 7th of June Lord Chelmsford was at Nondanai River, where a fortified post had been established. The 5th of June was the date of Colonel Buller's skirmish, already referred to, in which Lancers and Dragoons were engaged. On the 17th of June a correspondent reports that Newdigate's forces were constantly occupied patrolling and shelling *kraals* and *dongas*, with no appreciable result. At this time the Zulus appeared in great force within sight of the camp at Luneberg. Newdigate's column then marched to join that of General Wood. The utmost possible precautions were taken against surprise, both on the march and in camp.

At one place the rocks, which would have offered excellent cover for an attacking force, were mined. The mines could be fired by means of electricity from the laager. Lines of galvanized wire were also placed round the camp, which the soldiers styled "Cetywayo catchers." The heliograph vas used for signalling by means of flashes, and tamed out extremely useful. On the 26th of June[2] the 1st Brigade, with the Naval

---

2. It was in June that Lord Chelmsford received from the Secretary of State for War congratulations on the success of Ghinghelova, which he states he is convinced is largely due to the careful arrangements made by Lord Chelmsford for the march of the relieving column. He also says that the tenacity with which Ekowe was held by Colonel Pearson and the force under his command, deserves the highest praise. The Secretary for War, referring to the action with Wood's column, says, "I note with great satisfaction the part taken by the colonial troops in the operations, though I deeply regret the heavy losses they have sustained. The country has to deplore the loss of many gallant officers. It is difficult to single out individuals for special notice, but I most express my sorrow at the loss of Mr. Piet Uys, whose services on this as well as other occasions have been so fully recognized by those under whom he has served."

He also says, "Colonel Wood's force seems to have defended Kambula camp with a gallantry and determination worthy of great praise. I rejoice to note that the repulse of the enemy was on both occasions complete and decisive. I have communicated to the Queen the welcome news convoyed in Colonel Bellairs' telegram above referred to; and I have received her Majesty's commands to convey to you, and to the forces under your command, a gracious message of congratulation."

Brigade, moved from Fort Napoleon, and the long-expected junction of the columns appeared at last likely to be effected. It was certainly high time. The English imported horses in Newdigate's[3] brigade were beginning to suffer from the severity of weather and a scarcity of food, the Zulus had abundance of time to collect a large army, and the immense delay in striking a decisive blow discouraged our troops, encouraged the enemy, and caused immense dissatisfaction to the public at home and in the colony.

The Imperial Ministry at last seemed to partially yield to public pressure and public opinion. Sir Garnet Wolseley was appointed commander-in-chief and her Majesty's High Commissioner for the Natal, Transvaal, and Zululand. In connection with the homing questions of the day and the blame so lavishly bestowed upon the civil and military leaders in South Africa, the following despatch from the Secretary of State ought to be read with careful attention. Sir Michael Hicks Beach says (28th May, 1879) :—

After full consideration of the condition of affairs in South Africa, her Majesty's Government have decided that the arrangements under which the chief civil and military authority in the

---

3. A correspondent from Newdigate's column writes as follows:—"*Réveille* at 6 a.m. as usual; the men dispersed at 6.30 to drink the warm coffee prepared for them. Shortly after the disperse was sounded, to the annoyance of everyone in camp, the enjoyment of their coffee was spoilt by the assembly being sounded; the tents were lowered, the cavalry saddling up and riding some 200 yards from camp. The utility of this manoeuvre was not apparent to the troops, being at an unreasonable time. In Wood's column the alarm is invariably sounded about sunset after a new *laager* has been formed, in order that everyone might know at night what wagon he is stationed at, without creating confusion. If a night attack should be made, everything is so slovenly and loosely carried out here that we pray for the return of General Wood, to rejoin our own column; for then we feel that we should be safer from our enemies than we are from our friends. This column has too much gold lace and red tape about it for South African warfare. The contrast between the two columns is very striking in many things, more especially in the punctilious military etiquette of this column, where on every *aide* one is likely to be stopped by the sentry, and told that you must not go through a row of huts because a staff tent is under his charge. At headquarters, plebeian's feet most not intrude within a certain distance. With General Wood's column there are no sentries over staff tents; the only day sentries are over Government stores, the regimental colours, and guard tents. All the staff tents display flags, denoting that business is done there, and they are open to the approach of everyone who may have business to transact. General Wood, Colonel Bolter, and their officers, have no pride or affectation. As a rule the officers of all branches of the service follow the example at their commanders, and are as courteous and friendly as they are brave."

neighbourhood of the seat of war is distributed among four different persons can no longer be deemed adequate to the requirements of the present juncture.

2. In the number of imperial troops engaged, and the expenditure incurred, the Zulu war has assumed dimensions far exceeding those of any that has been carried on for many years in South Africa; and it appears but too evident that military operations have been seriously impeded by a want of harmony between the civil and military authorities, of which the difference that has arisen between the Lieutenant-General commanding the forces and the Lieutenant-Governor of Natal, with regard to the disposal of a portion of the native levies called out for service, has furnished a striking example.

3. In such a matter the High Commissioner has no power to interfere, but were it otherwise you would be unable, in present circumstances, to interfere with any practical effect. For the prompt action requisite in time of war would entirely preclude the satisfactory reference to Cape Town of this or any other of the numerous questions requiring the decision of the High Commissioner; while, on the other hand, your own presence at the seat of war has become impossible. After an unavoidable protracted absence from Cape Town (during which you have laboured with singular zeal and energy to discharge all the duties which have devolved upon you) you will be entirely occupied with many important matters necessarily postponed until your return.

4. The union of Griqualand West with the Cape, to the settlement of which your recent visit to the province will have largely contributed, has to be completed; the financial questions jointly concerning the colony and this country demand immediate attention; and important work remains to be done in carrying out the recent legislation of the Cape Parliament for the defence of the colony. But above all Her Majesty's Government are anxious that the larger and more complicated questions connected with confederation, on which I shall shortly address you, should be considered, under your guidance, during the approaching session of the Cape Parliament, and they attach special importance to the advantages which may be derived from your exertions in promoting this great work.

5. Under these circumstances, her Majesty's Government have determined to place the chief military and civil command in the eastern portion of South Africa in the hands of one officer, and they have selected Lieutenant-General Sir Garnet Wolseley, G.C.M.G., for this duty. His high professional standing and his varied and distinguished services preclude any question as to the fitness of placing him for the time in supreme authority over the able men now commanding her Majesty's troops in South Africa and administering the Governments of Natal and the Transvaal, and it is. equally beyond question that he will receive their most loyal and cordial support. Sir Garnet Wolseley will, in addition to his military command, be commissioned as Governor of Natal and of the Transvaal, and High Commissioner for Native and Foreign Affairs to the northward and eastward of those colonies.

In the latter capacity he will assume for the time that portion of your functions which, at a crisis of each gravity as the present, could not be performed by any High Commissioner acting at a distance of more than 1000 miles from the scene of operations. You will, I am confident, be the first to recognize the necessity of the arrangement, and will readily assist Sir Garnet Wolseley, should yon have returned to Cape Town by the time of his arrival there on his way to enter upon the duties of his office, with all the valuable information which your knowledge and experience enable you to afford.

The Under-Secretary for War, writing to Lord Chelmsford (29th May), says:—

I have now to convey to yon the intimation that her Majesty's Government, having carefully considered the information at their command, have come to the conclusion that the satisfactory administration of affairs in that part of South-Eastern Africa in the immediate neighbourhood of the seat of war can at the present moment only be carried out by placing that administration in the hands of one person holding plenary powers, both civil and military, and that they have selected Sir Garnet Wolseley to discharge these duties.

The Colonial Office will by this mail have informed Sir Bartle Frere of this decision, and of its effects so far as he himself is concerned.

With respect to the military command, though I have the satisfaction of informing you that it is not intended that the supersession caused by the appointment as High Commissioner of an officer senior to yourself should be considered as conveying censure on your proceedings, it will nevertheless be your duty, as in the ordinary course of service, to submit and to subordinate your plans to his control. This decision was communicated to you by telegram sent yesterday *via* St. Vincent, of which I enclose a copy.

Sir Garnet Wolseley, being qualified to act in a political as well as in a military capacity, will be in possession up to the latest date and in the fullest detail of the views of her Majesty's Government; the responsibility placed upon yon by Sir Bartle Frere with regard to the enforcement of his demands upon Cetywayo will therefore terminate upon the arrival of the High Commissioner, and any overtures for peace will henceforward he transmitted for decision by him.

The news of Sir Garnet Wolseley's appointment was received with the greatest satisfaction in South Africa. The campaign had reached a very critical stage, and the most contradictory and blundering reports about the attitude of the Zulus were constantly circulated. Cetywayo had been trying to deceive and gain time by sending in messages for peace. Lord Chelmsford, as a preliminary, had asked that the guns taken at Isandhlwana[4] should be returned. At the same time that Cetywajo pretended to desire peace, his people raided over our border at Middle Drift, swooped down upon the friendly natives near Luneberg, and endeavoured to enter into an alliance with rebellious Boers. The *impi* that had been occupying the Intombe valley was withdrawn into Zululand, and it was clear that a concentration of forces was about to take place at Ulundi.

Sir Garnet Wolseley arrived at Natal on the 27th of June. His staff comprised Colonels Colley, Russell, and Brackenbury; Major McCalmont; and Captains Lord Gifford, Bushman, Yeatman Biggs, Maurice, Brathwaite and Doyle. The Mayor and Corporation of D'Urban presented an address to his Excellency, in which, after heartily welcoming

---

4. On the 27th of June, Major-General Clifford telegraphs, "Black wires from Isandhlwana, 'I have just completed burying the dead; the outlying bodies may remain, but all those on the field of battle are now interred. The few remaining bodies far down on the Fugitives' Drift track will be interred in a day or two,'" Subsequently another party was sent, and suitable cairns were erected.

him, it is stated that British South Africa had unanimously endorsed the consistent policy adopted and pursued by Sir Bartle Frere, as the only means open for securing a lasting and honourable peace. Sir Garnet Wolseley, in returning thanks, expressed a hope that a strong and stable peace might be gained, as a means to secure lasting immunity from external discord and hostility. "Severe as is this stress upon you, you must, I feel confident, see cause for satisfaction in the patriotic and successful exertions with which your volunteers have laboured to avert peril from your country, and to maintain the prowess of English arms in battle."

The new General and High Commissioner then proceeded to Pietermaritzburg, and shortly afterwards returned and went by sea to Port Durnford, but being unable to land there, was compelled to return to D'Urban, and to proceed thence overland to the front.

A difference of opinion existed from the first as to the necessity of the Zulu war, and with reference to the character of Cetywayo. This became much more pronounced after the disaster at Isandhlwana. It is a significant fact that a very small minority of those who knew the Zulus and lived in Natal shared the sentiments of the British philanthropists, who lived securely at home, and took upon themselves to condemn a policy with the reasons for which they were only imperfectly acquainted. The Bishop of Natal, Dr. Colenso, was, in South Africa, the leader of the party who denounced the war. In the Blue Books laid before Parliament interesting letters from his able pen are published, in which he argues the Zulu case exactly as if the race were a civilized one, which could be expected to observe treaties, and with whom perfidy and deceit were unknown.

In a despatch from Sir Bartle Frere, written from Pretoria, in the Transvaal, and dated the 18th of April, the High Commissioner sums up the arguments for war. These reasons utterly and completely exclude any feeling or desire for vengeance, and all intention to advance civilization, commerce, and Christianity by the sword. It was absolutely necessary, however, that the Zulu king should cease to reign, the military power of that nation he broken up, and his people made to feel themselves subject to the British power. Sir Bartle Frere says:—

I believe that this is in the interests of the Zulus, no less than of their neighbours.

It is in the interest of the European population of Natal and the Transvaal, because they cannot possibly live in peace and quiet with the Zulus in their present state as neighbours.

The events of the last few months have rendered it unnecessary to prove by argument that the Zulus have been made into a great military power; that they can destroy an English regiment, with artillery to support it; or shut up or defeat a brigade six times as strong as the ordinary garrison of Natal, unless our troops are very carefully posted and very well handled.

The open declarations of their king, no less than the fundamental laws of their organization, proclaim foreign conquest and bloodshed as a necessity of their existence.

They are practically surrounded by British territory. Except the Portuguese, there is now no foreign territory they can reach for purposes of bloodshed without passing through British territory.

It is, therefore, clear that they cannot continue in their present condition, with their present form of government and present military organization, without attacking British subjects, or, at best, unoffending neighbours, who believe themselves safe as British subjects or allies.

They make no prisoners save, occasionally, young women and half-grown children. They show no quarter, and give no chance to the wounded or disabled, disembowelling them at once.

They are separated from Natal by a river easily fordable for the greater part of the year, and not too wide to talk across at any time.

The boundary between them and the Transvaal is even more easily passed.

All these, I submit, are incontrovertible facts, proved by the well-known events of the past few months.

I know that there are educated men to be found, of great ability, who claim to be lovers of liberty and of right, and of their own species, who have lived long near the Zulus, and who say there is no danger to be apprehended from them if we let them alone; that Cetywayo is a well-meaning prince, quite within his own right in massacring his own subjects, and our soldiers, too, if they enter his territory; that all that is necessary to our own safety is to let the Zulu king alone, or if the English do not like that, to leave his neighbourhood.

Having lived now for many weeks within a couple of Zulu marches of the Zulu border, among sensible Englishmen, many of them men of great sagacity, coolness, and determination, and reasonably just and upright in all their dealings, who never went to sleep without having their arms within reach, and being prepared to take refuge with wives and families at a minute's warning within a fortified post; having learnt from '*voortrekkers*' and their children, who had witnessed the massacres of Weenen and Blauwkrantz, and who could thus testify that the present peculiarities of Zulu warfare are no recent innovation; I may be allowed to doubt the possibility of making life within reach of a Zulu '*impi*' permanently tolerable to ordinary Englishmen and Dutchmen.

Nor does it seem to me that we can justly say to colonists, either in Natal or the Transvaal, that if they do not like the situation they may go elsewhere.

The Zulu right to be where the Zulus now are is, with the exception of a small and remote tract towards Delagoa Bay, simply one of recent conquest by devastation and massacre.

I have never heard the historical fact questioned that the earlier Zulu '*impis*' into what is now Natal and Transvaal territory preceded by a very few years, if they preceded at all, the first appearance of Dutch and English adventurers in the same lands; and the Zulus certainly cannot claim, as the Dutch and English may, any right of occupation from having civilized or improved the land.

Hence it seems to me no more than natural justice that if either party is to make way for the other, the Zulus should yield, and not the English or Dutch.

But I submit that in the interests of the Zulus themselves we have no right to leave them to their fate.

The present system of Cetywayo is no real choice of the nation. It is simply a reign of terror, such as has before now been imposed on some of the most civilized nations of the world. The people themselves are everything that could be desired as the unimproved material of a very fine race. They seem to have all the capacities for forming a really happy and civilized community, where law, order, and right shall prevail, instead of the present despotism of a ruthless savage.

I can imagine but three ways of their being so improved:—

1st. They might, living alongside a civilized community, gradually imbibe civilized ideas and habits.

But for this it is necessary that their civilized neighbours should be able to live in security, which, as I have already said, seems to me hopeless, unless the military organization and power of Cetywayo be broken down.

2nd. There are the means of improvement which may follow conquest and the breaking down of Cetywayo's military system; and this seems to me the only reasonable mode of doing our duty by these people. In the cases of Abyssinia and Ashantee we were compelled by circumstances to retire after conquest, and wash our hands of all further responsibility for the future of those countries; but there is no such necessity in the case of Zululand—there is nothing to prevent our taking up and easily carrying the burden of the duty laid upon us to protect and civilize it.

There is yet a third plan, which I have seen advocated by high authority.

The Zulus are, it is truly said, a nation of fine national characteristics. They have qualities which might enable them to become the regenerators and the foremost in civilization of all the nations in South Africa.

So far I can agree with those who hold the opinions I refer to, but not in their further belief that Cetywayo is the Attila of the Zulus, and that if we only let him alone he will develop into a Charlemagne or an Alfred.

How far this process might be rendered tolerable to the present civilized inhabitants of Natal and the Transvaal, I will not stop to inquire. It is quite possible that Zulus, overrunning their now civilized neighbours, might in due time imbibe some of their civilization, settle down, and become civilized themselves, absorbing through their captives and subjects the germs of a better system of national existence.

I may doubt the probability of such a result, but I will not contest its possibility, and will only say that I am quite sure the countrymen of the present settlers in Natal and the Transvaal will never leave the colonists there to be made the subjects of any such experiment.

I can, as I started by saying, see no alternative compatible with our duty but effectually to subdue the Zulus, and govern them as other South African races subject to the British Crown are governed.

It seems to me that no terms can possibly be made with Cety-wayo which can be compatible with such a result, save with the indispensable preliminary of his entire submission.

In the beginning of July Lord Chelmsford's column was with-in ten miles of the king's *kraal* at Ulundi. Messengers again arrived from Cetywayo, and on this occasion they brought the sword of the Prince Imperial as a peace offering. The amanuensis of Cetywayo was a Dutchman, named Vogel, who took the opportunity of marking in pencil on the envelope of the letter, that the king had 20,000 men with him. The reply of Lord Chelmsford was as follows:—

If the *induna*, Mandula, brings with him the 1000 rifles taken at Isandhlwana, I will not insist on 1000 men coming in to lay down their arms, if the Zulus are afraid to come. He must bring the two guns and the remainder of the cattle. I will then be willing to negotiate. As he has caused me to advance by the great delay he has made, I must now go to the Umvolosi to enable my men to drink. I will consent, pending negotiations, to halt on the further bank of the river, and will not burn any *kraals* until the 3rd of July, provided no opposition is made to my advance to the position on the Umvolosi, by which day, the 3rd of July, at noon, the conditions must be complied with. If my force is fired on, I shall consider negotiations are at an end, and to avoid any chance of this, it is best that Mundula come to my camp at daybreak or tonight, and that the Zulus, should withdraw from the neighbourhood of the river to Ulundi. I cannot stop the general in command of the coast army until these conditions are complied with."

Of course, nothing more was seen or heard of Mundula. On the 2nd of July an *impi*, 20,000 strong, advanced from Ulundi as if to at-tack. Newdigate and Wood, at a short distance from each other, imme-diately *laagered* their wagons, and these preparations seemed to check the enemy. It is possible that Cetywayo had personally some idea of surrendering, as it is stated that a large herd of white cattle (the royal colour) was seen coming towards the camp from the direction of Ce-tywayo's new stronghold at Mahize Kanye. A number of men came out and drove the cattle back. A sudden scare or panic had just taken place at the camp. Men of the Native Contingent, having become alarmed, rushed in over a portion of the 2-4th Regiment; our short-service red jackets, seeing naked black men rushing in past them, *as-*

segai in hand, imagined that the Zulus were upon them, and fled in terror within the *laager*. So demoralized did the men become, that it required the exertion of physical force on the part of their officers to induce them to return to their posts.

On the 3rd of July a large force of mounted men, under Colonel Buller, crossed the river at a drift commanded by a rocky hill, from which the enemy were gallantly and quickly dislodged by Baker's Irregular Horse. Buller moved forward to Nodwengu Kraal, and on the way several stragglers were killed. One of them was "stuck" by Lord William Beresford, with the exclamation, "First spear, by Jove!" Shortly afterwards this force was nearly trapped, by means of the decoy of a man with a number of goats, who moved forward in front. The nonchalance of this fellow was so suspicions, that the force was suddenly wheeled to the right in the direction of Ulundi; and no sooner was this done than a crowd of Zulus, who had been in ambush, rose out of a *donga* at a hundred yards distance, and poured in a heavy volley. Preparations for battle were made during the night of the 3rd of July. War-dancing took place among the enemy, while on our side the wagons were carefully formed into *laager*, and at 6 a.m. on the 4th of July, the British army, leaving this camp, crossed the Umvolosi River, and ascending to the high ground, formed upon it in order of battle.

The following graphic description of the pursuit of stragglers, and a narrow escape from falling into a Zulu trap, will be read with interest—"During the first two days the king made no sign, and his people were marching, drilling, and performing war dances in a fashion that did not strike me as being very pacific. On the day the armistice expired at noon (July 3rd), the question was solved in a way that most at least have convinced even Lord Chelmsford himself, that Cetywayo had been making a fool of him. Early in the morning (about 9 a.m.), lurking Zulus crept down to the strong *kopje* commanding; the drift, and fired on the soldiers, who were washing and bathing in the river below.

There was a great panic and scamper, but I believe no one was wounded. That, however, was not all, for some of them came across the river and drove off fifty trek oxen which were feeding, taking them over the river and some distance op the opposite bank. The cattle guard promptly crossed and recaptured them, but up to noon our camp was insulted by the impudent rascals firing at as, and some few of the Martini-Henry bullets actually fell in the camp and *laager*. This was carrying things too far, and at noon Buller's brigade was ordered out to try and cut off a few of them. We crossed the river at a drift below the camp, and galloping round the base of the hill, tried to pick off a few; but we were too late. They had seen our preparations and were off, and we saw them racing off near Nodwengu.

We started in pursuit, and on nearing the *kraal* we overtook the rear fugitive. There was a race to get him, amongst half a dozen of us, but he fell to Lord William Beresford, who gave point with his sabre, just as the Zulu turned to use his *assegai*, running him through the shield and through the body. We then turned and galloped after the others, at least 150, whom we should have cut off had everything been on the square; but the black rascals were leading us into a nice trap, which had been laid for the express purpose. Half-way between Nodwengu and Ulundi there is a sluggish *spruit*, with a deep bed, which runs parallel with this road for some distance, and then turns sharply across it at right angles.

I had doubts when I saw some of these fugitives disappear in the *spruit* bed, and these doubts became certainty when I heard Buller shout out to 'retire,' and almost at the same moment, before we could get our horses up and round, two lines of Zulus rose in the *spruit* bed and poured in a volley within 100 yards. It they had known how to shoot, which happily for us they do not, nearly every saddle ought to have been emptied; but only three men and half a dozen horses were over. Lord William Beresford took up a dismounted man, and Commandant D'Arcy one who was wounded. The former got his man out safety; the latter, I am sorry to say, was thrown by his horse bucking at the unaccustomed burden.

The poor trooper was overtaken and killed, while the commandant was so severely bruised from falling on his revolver, that he was able to get back safe, but not able to take part in the next day's fight. It is hardly necessary to say that we galloped back at least as fast as we had come, perhaps even a little faster, for we were seen and pursued, Zulus springing up from the grass in all directions and firing continuously. We ran the gauntlet the whole way back, making only one rally on a crest sprinkled with small trees. The line in our rear was 500 yards off, and some of them were shot, but we were not able to stop very long, for we saw columns making for the drift to cut us off.

Happily Colonel Buller had left Baker and his men on the stony *kopje* to cover our retreat, and his men peppered one of these intercepting columns so effectually as to stop their advance. Our peril was seen from the camp, and Major Le Grice's battery of 9-pounders took up a position on the high ground in front, from which they so astonished the other column of Zulus by a well-directed fire of shrapnel at long range, that they too were prevented from carrying out their philanthropic intention. We had only, therefore, the pursuing Zulus to deal with, but they followed up closely as far as the ford, where Captain Whalley, with the Natal Light Horse, drew up and covered our crossing. It is a marvel to me, considering the heavy fire that we were under, that we only lost three men killed, four wounded, and thirteen horses missing."

It was here that the Zulus had defeated the Boers, and it was, therefore, fitting that upon the field where the white men had met with disaster their crowning triumph should take place. A victory sufficient to repair and efface the stains of all previous calamities was absolutely required, and it was obtained in the most complete and satisfactory manner.

The leaders of the Zulu army were named Tyingwayo, Manyamane, Dabulamanzi, Mondola, Sirayo, Mehkla Ka Zulu. The force under their command numbered more than thirteen corps of regiments, was larger than that at Kambula, and comprised more than 20,000 men. One of the prisoners, named Undungunyanga, son of Umgegane, declared that it was true the king had wanted to make peace, and previous to the battle, in an address to the army, said that as the Inkandampeonvui regiment would not let the white cattle go to the British as a peace offering, and as the white army was now at his home, they could fight. The battle was to take place on the open plain between the Nodwengu and Ulundi Kraals. The king then personally placed the different regiments, gave final orders, and retired to a *kraal* at a short distance to witness the battle.[5]

The place in which the British army was drawn up had many

5. This Zulu prisoner also stated, "The white man who writes the king's letters is a trader. The king has his movements always watched." Speaking of the result of the battle of Ulundi, he said, "The army is now thoroughly beaten, and, as we were beaten in the open, it will not reassemble or fight again."

advantages, A broad open country was around, almost free from bush. The Nodwengu Kraal, distant about 1000 yards, offered some cover to the enemy, and it would have been burned had not Colonel Buller suggested that if this were done the Zulus would be enabled to creep up under cover of the smoke.

Very shortly after a halt had been made, and while the solemn duty of burying one of our men, killed on the previous day, was taking place, it was observed that the enemy was approaching from the direction of Ulundi, and from the bush on the right. Our troops were formed up in a hollow parallelogram. In the centre was the Native Contingent, with ammunition wagons. The four sides of the parallelogram were formed by eight companies of the 13th Regiment, five companies of the 80th Regiment, the 90th, 58th, and 34th Regiments, together with the 17th Lancers and the mounted irregulars. At the corners and centres artillery was placed—Gatlings,[6] 7-pounders, and 9-pounders.

At half-past 8 a.m., as the enemy were advancing, Buller's mounted men were thrown out on the front, left, and rear. As the right was left uncovered by cavalry, Cochrane's Mounted Basutos were sent out from this direction to make the enemy advance nearer. As they retired the right face of the square commenced the action by a brisk fire. At ten minutes to nine o'clock the attacking army was so near the British as to make the fire from the latter become general. Silently and steadily the horns of the Zulu army came on in their usual manner; without a word or cry, the warriors of Cetywayo continued to press forward in spite of the deadly fusillade.

As at Ghinghelovo and Kambula, so now at Ulundi, their extraordinary bravery and contempt of death was the chief feature in the attack. During this time the British infantry were formed in four ranks, of which the front knelt, while the rear rank was reversed. Inside the square every means of obtaining ammunition swiftly was provided. The continuous and tremendous fire poured upon the advancing enemy had no perceptible effect at first. On, like a wave of the sea which cannot be stopped, poured the human tide; but when it had advanced to a distance of seventy yards, flesh and blood could no longer stand the awful destruction which poured from the British lines.

The main body hesitated and stopped. A few, more intrepid than the others, rushed on; but the wavering feeling spread throughout the

6. The Gatlings were not very successful. Firing had to cease six times during the action, as they got overheated.

Zulu host, and now was the exact moment to take advantage of it. The dogs of war were suddenly slipped. Out rushed the Lancers, and bore down like a hurricane upon the disheartened and discouraged multitude. Shells were breaking in all directions among their masses, the incessant "pings" of rifle bullets were doing deadly execution; and when the cavalry plunged in among them, the Zulu army was literally torn asunder and broken. The flower of these warriors of Zululand made yet one wild effort, when Captain Edgell, of the Lancers, was shot dead, and Captain Drury-Lowe, Lieutenant James, and other officers had a narrow escape.

Nine men were killed, and no fewer than seventy-five were wounded. But all was in vain; Cetywayo's great army was forced to turn and fly. They had met the white man upon the open plain, and, though more than 20,000 to 5000, were totally and completely defeated. Away went the mounted men in pursuit, and before the slaughter ended, fully 1000 of the Zulu army bit the dust. The Lancers, with the Irregular Horse, did very good work, as it is estimated 450 of the enemy were killed in the pursuit. The Zulus ran with surprising swiftness. The Lancers drove a crowd into a *donga*, and working round, pursued a mass of fugitives, who, being overtaken and at bay, made an unavailing stand, when 160 of their number were killed.

A rest was ordered after the battle; and then the mounted force rode on to Ulundi, which was found wholly deserted, and was at once given to the flames. Subsequently all the forces fell back upon the laagered camp which had been left in the morning. Ulundi, the great place of the great monarch of Southern Africa, was wholly destroyed. The king's palace consisted merely of a thatched building of four rooms with a verandah. A Spartan absence of all furniture and of all luxuries was perceptible, but the numerous huts and *kraals* indicated that this place had been the headquarters of a powerful army. Lord William Beresford was the first to enter.

It was a grand sight to see the flames mounting to the skies, and to know that in their smoke the prestige and influence of the greatest savage power in Southern Africa had ended. Mr. Archibald Forbes, the correspondent of the *Daily News*, although suffering from a wound, galloped to the colony with the news of this victory. He carried an important despatch from the general, and was the first to telegraph the news to Natal and to the world. Starting early in the forenoon, immediately after the battle of Ulundi, he rode in fourteen hours a distance of 110 miles to the nearest telegraph station at Landman's Drift, on the Buffalo River. Twice he lost his way in the midst of dense mist, and during the entire journey he was exposed to attack by scattered parties of the enemy. It was a daring ride, which will live in history, and deserved special and generous recognition.

The following is hard Chelmsford's telegraphic despatch giving a description of the battle:—

Cetywayo not having complied with my demands by noon yesterday, July 3rd, and having fired heavily on the troops at the water, I returned the 114 cattle he had sent in, and ordered a reconnaissance to be made by the mounted force under Colonel Buller; this was effectually made, and caused the Zulu army to advance and show fight.

This morning, a force under my command, consisting of the second division, under Major-General Newdigate, numbering 1870 Europeans, 530 natives, and eight guns, and the flying column under Brigadier-General Wood, numbering 2192 Europeans, 578 natives, four guns, and two Gatlings, crossed the Umvolosi River at 6.15, and marching in a hollow square, with the ammunition and entrenching tool carts and bearer company in its centre, reached an excellent position between Nodwengu and Ulundi, about half-past 8 a.m. This had been observed by Colonel Buller the day before.

Our fortified camp on the right banks of the Umvolosi river was left with a garrison of about 900 Europeans, 250 natives, and one Gatling gun, under Colonel Bellairs.

Soon after half-past seven the Zulu army was seen leaving its bivouacs and advancing on every side. The engagement was shortly afterwards commenced by the mounted men.

By nine o'clock the attack was fully developed. At half-past nine the enemy wavered; the 17th Lancers, followed by the remainder of the mounted men, attacked them, and a general rout ensued.

The prisoners state that Cetywayo was personally commanding and had made all the arrangements himself, and that he witnessed the fight from Qikarzi Kraal, and that twelve regiments took part in it. If so, 20,000 men attacked us.

It is impossible to estimate with any correctness the loss of the enemy, owing to the extent of country over which they attacked and retreated, but it could not have been less, I consider, than 1000 killed. By noon Ulundi was in flames, and during the day all military *kraals* of the Zulu army and in the valley of the Umvolosi were destroyed. At 2 p.m. the return march to the camp of the column commenced.

The behaviour of the troops under my command was extremely satisfactory; their steadiness under a complete belt of fire was remarkable. The dash and enterprise of the mounted branches was all that could be wished, and the fire of the artillery very good. A portion of the Zulu force approached our fortified camp, and at one time threatened to attack it. The Native Contingent, forming a part of the garrison, were sent out after the action, and assisted in the pursuit.

As I have fully accomplished the object for which I advanced, I consider I shall now be best carrying out Sir Garnet Wolseley's instructions by moving at once to Entonganini, and thence to Kwamagaza. I shall send back a portion of this force with empty wagons, for supplies, which are now ready at Fort Marshall.

The last paragraph of this despatch requires comment. A great victory had been gained, and certainly should have been improved upon. It was known that Cetywayo was with the army, and subsequent intelligence proved that a very little effort would have resulted in his capture. The new *kraal* of the king was only twelve miles distant, and if a forward movement had been made to that place, an enormous advantage, which was merely a logical sequence of the battle, could have been secured. Sir Garnet Wolseley's instructions about retiring to Entonganini are quoted, and he is apparently made responsible for a retrograde step. Thus was the war still further protracted in an unnecessary manner. As regards the battle of Ulundi itself. Lord Chelmsford did not attack, but was attacked. Both at home and in the colonies, throughout the Empire, there was a generous thrill of joy among all classes, not only for the decisive victory, but because it had been gained by a general who had been previously so unfortunate.[7]

The beginning of the end had now arrived, and evident signs were

---

7 Sir Garnet Wolseley was at dinner at Fort Pearson when the news of the victory of Ulundi was received, and a correspondent who was present thus describes its reception:—"As we sat at dinner we discussed all the probabilities and possibilities of the situation. Had Lord Chelmsford embarked upon a desperate enterprise of his own? What if success should not be his? And when we thought of Isandhlwana our reflections were gloomy. We were still at dinner when a despatch was handed to Sir Garnet, and as he read it his face broke into a smile, and looking up cheerfully he said, 'This is indeed the best news I have read for many a long day. (Cont. next page.)

not wanting that the Zulus accepted their defeat at Ulundi as a settlement of the question of supremacy. Lord Chelmsford resigned, and proceeded with a large staff from Entonganini to Pietermaritzburg. On this long journey he met not the slightest attempt at interruption or any sign of hostility. No enemy lurked in the Umhlatusi Bush, and in every direction the Zulus could be seen rebuilding their huts and cultivating their fields. The sword was turned into the ploughshare, and the ruling of fate was submitted to. Still serious doubts filled the minds of old colonists, who ranked above all their other qualities the supreme cunning and dissimulation of the Zulu race. It was felt as a calamity that no forward move had been made after Ulundi, and that there was no real finality to the war, until Cetyvajo was either killed or captured.

Lord Chelmsford arrived at the capital of Natal on the 21st of July, and was received there with an enthusiasm which completely surprised him. Powerful reactions are common in the public mind, and the general who had yesterday been severely criticized, was today lauded to the skies. The Corporation presented an address in which it was made a source of special gratification that, after the numerous unforeseen difficulties which had to be overcome, his lordship's arms had obtained a brilliant and decisive victory. At D'Urban a grand public banquet was given, when Sir Garnet Wolseley, Sir Henry Bulwer, General Clifford, Sir Evelyn Wood, Colonel Buller, and all distinguished officers and citizens were present.

Lord Chelmsford on this occasion said,:

There is a saying very frequently quoted now-a-days, that *nothing succeeds like success*, but, gentlemen, if I thought that you asked me to dinner simply because I had been successful, it would be as water from the Dead Sea placed to my mouth; but from what the Mayor has said, it is clear you sympathize with me not because I succeeded, but because under circumstances

---

Tonight, gentlemen, we may sleep peacefully, for Lord Chelmsford has been engaged with the army of the Zulu king, and has thoroughly defeated it." The despatch was from Mr. Sivewright, the general manager of the telegraph in South Africa. Sir Garnet read us the sentence, short, clear, and decisive, showing us how Cetjwayo in person had made his final effort to save his kingdom, and was now a refugee and an outcast from his nation in the black swamps of the Umvolosi. The despatch was read by order of the general to the troops; and borne by the high wind across the waters of the Tugela into Zululand went the British cheers which announced the fall of the bold, brave, cruel, and crafty king. We slept soundly that night."

of extreme difficulty I endeavoured to do my duty. There have been many painful incidents connected with the war, so that it is impossible to look back upon it without mingled feelings of satisfaction and regret. On this I will not further touch; but there is one point on which I can look back with pure and unalloyed satisfaction, already alluded to by my gallant friend General Wood—I mean the loyal and efficient assistance given to me by all ranks in the army, which is such that the satisfaction and pride that I feel will be remembered as long as I live.

I never could have believed it possible for any general to receive such assistance and devotion as I have experienced from my men. I could always feel that, whether I was present or absent, they were striving to do their best to get out of difficulties, and this was not confined to one rank, but was common to all ranks; and I believe I may say that I had the confidence and sincere support of all ranks of the army, from the lowest to the highest.

It would be invidious to particularize individuals and services, but when I look back eighteen months, two names stand out in broad relief—those already alluded to, the one by the Mayor, and the other by General Wood—the names of Wood and Buller. I can say that these two have been my right and left supporters during the whole of my time in this country. They came out with me in the same steamer; in every position I have been in they have been in the forefront, and now I feel proud to think they return with me to their native land again.

The Mayor asked one question, namely, whether the war was over or not. I think I can best answer this by saying that these two men are going back to England; depend upon it, if there were any great work to be done, these two men would never have left the forces. I again thank you for the manner in which you have drank this toast, and desire to include in my thanks all those who met me on Monday night. I shall carry back a grateful remembrance of this place; and if in the public position I shall hold it is ever possible for me to render any assistance towards the prosperity of the colony, you may depend upon it I shall do so.

In concluding this chapter, it seems right to quote fully from the London *Gazette* the official reasons for placing five brave men on, the "roll of fame" for gallant deeds performed in the Zulu war.

The Queen has been graciously pleased to signify her intention to confer the decoration of the Victoria Cross on the under-mentioned officers and soldier of her Majesty's army, whose claims have been submitted for her Majesty's approval, for their gallant conduct during the recent operations in South Africa, as recorded against their names, *viz*,:—

Captain and Brevet Lieutenant-Colonel Redvers H. Buller, C.B., 60th Rifles, for his gallant conduct at the retreat at Zlobane on the 28th of March, 1879, in having assisted, while hotly pursued by Zulus, in rescuing Captain C. D'Arcy, of the Frontier Light Horse, who was retiring on foot, and carrying him on his horse until he overtook the rearguard. Also for having, on the same date and under the same circumstances, conveyed Lieutenant C. Everitt, of the Frontier Light Horse, whose horse had been killed under him, to a place of safety. Later on Colonel Buller, in the same manner, saved a trooper of the Frontier Light Horse, whose horse was completely exhausted, and who otherwise would have been killed by the Zulus, who were within eighty yards of him.

Major William K. Leet, lst Battalion, 13th Regiment, for his gallant conduct on the 28th of March, 1879, in rescuing from the Zulus Lieutenant A. M. Smith, of the Frontier Light Horse, during the retreat from the Zlobane. Lieutenant Smith, while on foot, his horse having been shot, was closely pursued by the Zulus, and would have been killed, had not Major Leet taken him upon his horse and rode with him, under the fire of the enemy, to a place of safety.

Surgeon-Major James Henry Reynolds, Army Medical Department, for the conspicuous bravery, during the attack at Rorke's Drift, on the 22nd and 23rd of January, 1879, which he exhibited in his constant attention to the wounded under fire, and in his voluntarily conveying ammunition from the store to the defenders of the hospital, whereby he exposed himself to a cross fire from the enemy, both in going and returning.

Lieutenant Edward S. Browne, 1st Battalion, 24th Regiment, for the gallant conduct on the 29th of March, 1879, when the Mounted Infantry were being driven in by the enemy at Zlobane, in galloping back and twice assisting on his horse (under heavy fire and within a few yards of the enemy) one of the mounted men, who most otherwise have fallen into the enemy's hands.

Private Wassall, 80th Regiment, for his gallant conduct in having, at the imminent risk of his own life, saved that of Private Westwood, of the same regiment. On the 22nd of January, 1879, when the camp at Isandhlwana was taken by the enemy. Private Wassail retreated towards the Buffalo River, in which he saw a comrade struggling and apparently drowning. He rode to the bank, dismounted, leaving his horse on the Zulu side, rescued the man from the stream, and again mounted his horse, dragging Private Westwood across the river, under a heavy shower of bullets.

CHAPTER 10

The Hunt and Capture of Cetywayo

Before leaving the shores of South Africa, Lord Chelmsford took occasion at Cape Town to make a public defence of his policy, an which he denied that he had been guilty of hesitation and vacillation. His mind was made up at a very early date, and he went on unswervingly to Ulundi by the route he had originally resolved upon. If the work were to be done over again he would adopt the same plan of campaign. In marching upon Ulundi no calculation was made for assistance from the coast column—only indirect support was reckoned upon. After the crashing defeat at Ulundi no advantage would have been gained by endeavouring to penetrate the difficult country lying north of the king's *kraal*, even had the state of supplies permitted it.

While, therefore, one portion of the force retraced its steps towards the Blood River, escorting the sick and wounded, and taking with it all the empty wagons, the others moved *via* Kwamagwasa to St. Paul's, and then completed the chain of strongly entrenched posts extending east and west along the centre of Zululand at intervals of about twenty miles. So far one side of the question. On the other hand, men of unquestioned ability and experience, correspondents for several of the leading journals of the world, did not hesitate to blame Lord Chelmsford severely. These men were on the spot, were qualified to form an opinion, and it is absurd and unjust to imagine that political bias of any sort guided their pens.

The *Times'* correspondent complains of the want of a definite plan, and speaks of orders having been countermanded, and of general uncertainty. "What is wanted is a bolder determination."

On the 16th of June he writes, "We are wandering towards Ulundi much as the children of Israel wandered towards Canaan, without plans or even definite notions for the future. Plain, commonsense plans suffice, if backed by energy, decision, and determination."

The *Telegraph's* correspondent tells us that Lord Chelmsford's intelligence department "has been singularly defective throughout."

The correspondent of the *Daily News*, Mr. Archibald Forbes, thoroughly shared these opinions, and expresses them with conspicuous power and ability. Indeed, it is almost impossible for anyone to study carefully the proceedings of this protracted campaign, from the arrival of reinforcements in March until the battle of Ulundi, and not come to conclusions by no means complimentary to the general commanding-in-chief. It is urged that carriers, such as those employed by Sir Garnet Wolseley immediately after his arrival,[1] would have immensely facilitated transport, and when we consider that 4000 British troops at Ulundi defeated, in the open field, the concentrated power of Cetywayo—an army of more than 20,000 men—it is hard to believe that a column such as Wood's, properly reinforced and moving quickly, would not have been able to finish the war.

Sir Garnet Wolseley's proceedings were of the most prompt and vigorous character. Disappointed in not being able to land at Port Durnford, he had to return to D'Urban and proceed overland to General Crealock's coast column. When near the coast, he was gratified by receiving news of the battle of Ulundi, but was subsequently disappointed at Lord Chelmsford's neglecting to take full advantage of this victory. That officer almost immediately resigned, and had an interview with Sir Garnet, whom he met at St. Paul's. A Ulundi column was organized under Lieutenant-Colonel Clarke, consisting of the 60th Regiment, Barrow's Mounted Infantry, two troops of Lonsdale's Horse, and two troops of the Native Contingent.

This small movable column was ordered to operate towards the upper waters of the White and Black Umvolosi; Oham, with a *burgher* force, was to more from Luneberg. On the 21st of July Sir Garnet had a satisfactory interview with the principal Zulu chiefs. Dabulamanzi, the king's brother and one of the chief leaders of his army, had

---

1. "Some 2000 Zulus have been employed by the general as carriers, on the same principle as he adopted in the Ashantee campaign. It has proved a great success, and saved tremendous expense in transport. They receive twenty shillings per month, and rations. Every man carries fifty-six pounds at a time. This system has caused some discontent among the Natal Native Contingent, who complain that after these men fighting against us the Government are paying and allowing them the same privilege as themselves. But considering these men don't do half the work the carriers do, and having a natural failing for grumbling, no notice is taken of their complaint."

surrendered at Fort Chelmsford (Crealock's column) on the 11th of July, and numbers of minor chiefs, with their people, came forward to declare their submission to the British Government. Colonel Baker Russell was directed to operate from Intabankawa, in the direction of the Black Umvolosi, lending assistance to Oham, whose forces were situated in a more northerly direction.

Under Colonel Villiers it was arranged that the Swazis should cross the Pongolo, accompanied by Political Agent Macleod. As Sir Garnet considered that there were more troops in the command than were necessary, the first division and cavalry brigade were broken up. Generals Crealock and Marshall went home. The 1-13th, 1-24th, and 17th Lancers were ordered to leave, and several colonial corps were disbanded. Brigadier-General Wood and Colonel Buller required rest, and proceeded to England, while the Marines who arrived by the *Jumna*, from Plymouth, were sent back before even they reached Natal.

The chase of Cetywayo must always form an interesting episode in British colonial history. No war in Zululand could be said to be thoroughly at an end in which the despot whose will was law throughout the entire country was left uncaptured. The task of securing his person was a very difficult one. The king was looked upon as sacred, and we shall see that the most unbounded loyalty was manifested towards him. The country into which he had retreated was broken and difficult, intersected by forests and unprovided with roads. Above all, the people were thoroughly hostile, and faithful unto death to the monarch who was pursued to death by the hated white man. Nevertheless, the chase was successful, and that it was so reflected immense credit upon those engaged in it.

The force told off for the duty was organized at Ulundi. It was placed under the command of Major Barrow, and comprised the King's Dragoon Guards, the Mounted Infantry, Lonsdale's Horse, Captain Norse's Mounted Contingent, Jantje's Horse under Captain Hayes, together with a corps of Guides under Corporal Acutt. The hunt lasted fourteen days, and commenced on a Tuesday afternoon with a forced march of twenty-one hours, during the whole of which time the men were in the saddle. In this manner Zonyamma's Kraal was reached, where it was supposed the king might be. The king had left the day previously with thirty men. Two hours' rest, and away over very hilly country.

A terribly steep hill was descended, and a *kraal* visited where Cetywayo had been that morning. The River Mona was then crossed, and a steep hill ascended in order to reach Umbopa's Kraal, where the scent was entirely lost. Of course, the Zulus knew where the king was, but nothing on earth would induce them to tell. Umbopa (whose son was with Cetywayo) was then made prisoner and taken to his son's *kraal*, at a distance of five miles, where some of the king's slaughter oxen were found.

The *kraal* was deserted. Lord Gifford, second in command, was then ordered to scour the country, and had a very exciting but unsuccessful chase after a naked Zulu, who afterwards turned out to be one of the king's servants, appointed to look out and give warning of the approach of pursuers. Forty Zulus were got together by Major Barrow, but neither promises nor threats had any effect upon them. They were as loyal to their sable ruler as a faithful Highlander to his chief, or a loyal Cavalier to his king. At last it was accidentally mentioned that one of Cetywayo's own servants was present. With great difficulty some information was obtained from him, and a promise to put the British force on the right track.

At the dawn of day the dense black forests of the Umvolosi were entered, and as they proceeded pots and *calabashes*, evidently dropped in flight, were picked up. On—on until the river was reached, but there, alas! the trail was completely wanting. A few "*koodoos*" quietly grazing was the only sign of life. Lord Gifford was then sent to Funwayo's Kraal, eight miles distant, and there information was obtained that some of the king's girls had been seen passing that way. Five miles further on was Shemana's Kraal, where the same party were again heard of. Pushing through thick bush and long grass, in which the small band under Lord Gifford—only eleven in number—could very easily have been cut off, they got at length to a *kraal*, where they again heard of the girls.

Thence, taking two men as guides, they proceeded further, taking care to make for the open country, in order to intercept Cetywayo in case he endeavoured to peach the Inkanhla Forest. At last they reached Umgitya's Kraal, from whence they could overlook the bush in which they supposed the king to be. Disappointment then met them on every side, only relieved by the encounter with the two girls who, in spite of emphatic denials , there was every reason to believe were the property of the king. One of the king's own servants was shortly afterwards captured, and inside his bundle was found a valuable Martini-Henry rifle of excellent workmanship. Subsequently, this prisoner confessed that he had left the king only two or three days previously.

A day's rest was then taken, and while encamped, seven girls, a young man, and a boy were caught, who reported that Cetywayo was captured, and that they had fled from his place two days before. It then turned out that when the pursuing party was encamped on the banks of the Black Umvolosi, they were only within 300 yards of the king, some of whose people ran away, thinking that his capture was certain. Next day they commenced to scour the bush. There they had to sleep, while Zulu beef and Zulu beer were their fare. Most of the party at this time thought the game was up, but Lord Gifford was still full of hope. Back they went, beating the bush on the way, to Umbopa's son's place, where the *kraal* was burned and the cattle captured.

The main body was shortly afterwards reached, and there, at last, rather precise information was obtained from a Zulu "by means of proper persuasive measures." This man was to act as guide, but no sooner had they entered the bush than he slipped off and escaped. Two places which had evidently been prepared for the king were seen, and the party had to return again to the *kraals*, which had now become headquarters.

Two of Oham's men came in professing their loyalty, and were appointed spies, but a little boy revealed the fact that one of them had been with the king down in the bush, and then, before all the people, they were told that their double-dealing and humbug were perfectly understood. Trails were followed, people were examined, but all to no purpose; fealty to the king was paramount. Neither the loss of their cattle, which were carried off, the fear of death, nor the offer of bribes, immense in value to them, were of any avail. Returning from one of their long exploring expeditions, a woman was suddenly met in the bush, whose fright at the sight of the white men and the guns was so great as to make her confess the place where the king had slept two nights previously.

A party went off at dusk to this place, and captured three brothers, who being questioned, under fear of death, declared that they knew nothing, and that if killed they would die innocently. In the dark forest, lit up by the moon and the bright glare of the bivouac fire, the three men stood before their captors. It was a subject worthy of the pencil of Salvator Rosa. Interrogatories, threats, promises, all were useless, until at last the plan was adopted of leading one of the brothers away blindfolded behind a bush, and causing a rifle to be fired off in such a way as to induce the others to believe that he was shot. At last, overcome by fear, one of them told where the king had slept the night before, and where he had seen him that morning.

The other brother, being informed that everything was known, confirmed the intelligence. Away went Lord Gifford and his party, with these two men as guides, and at daybreak the *kraal* was reached and found deserted. The direction that Cetywayo had taken was then pointed out, and having been followed to one of Umnyamna's *kraals*, it was then discovered that the king was only five miles distant, and had halted for the day. It was then absolutely necessary to surround the place without being seen, particularly as his refuge was close by the side of a forest, into which, upon the slightest alarm, he would immediately escape.

As it was known that the Dragoons had gone some distance beyond this place, a note was sent by Lord Gifford to Major Marter, telling him to watch the passes. The latter officer, upon questioning the Zulu, ascertained where the king was, and immediately made such dispositions as to render escape impossible. The *kraal* was surrounded before Cetywayo had the slightest idea that his pursuers were upon him. The men of the Natal Native Contingent called upon him to surrender, but no notice was taken of this summons. Upon Major Marter repeating it, the king came out. The natives stretched out their hands towards him, but with dignity the monarch of the Zulus waved them back, and surrendered to Major Marter, accompanying his submission with a request that he might be immediately shot. He was informed, in reply, that if no resistance were made his person was perfectly safe.

Then there was mounting in hot haste, and, under the escort of Major Marter's party, the king, with four of his women, were hurried away towards Ulundi. From that place an ambulance with eight mules was sent out, on the morning of the 29th of August, to proceed to the Black Umvolosi River and convey him thence. The king complained of the jolting, and walked a good deal of the way.

The authority for the preceding account is Mr. Lysight, interpreter with Lord Gifford's party. The following is the interesting narrative of the capture given by Major Marter. That officer left Colonel Clarke's column at the Black Umvolosi at daylight on Wednesday the 27th, in consequence of news coming in from General Colley that the king was making for the Ignome Forest. He had with him his squadron King's Dragoon Guards, one company of Barton's natives under Captain Plesh, ten Mounted Irregulars under Lieutenant Wingh, and young Oftenbro as interpreter, with four scouts or guides. He sent his men on to threaten the inhabitants of the *kraals* that unless they gave him information about the king and helped to catch him, he had orders to burn their *kraals*, take prisoners, capture cattle, and not allow them to cultivate any land until he was caught.

At last he got an indirect hint, after sleeping out one night, from a Zulu whom he met, named Uzililo, who stated that he had come from Umbopa's *kraal*, and had heard that the "wind blew that way," pointing to where the king was afterwards taken, but that the troops had better go "that way," pointing further to the north-east, so as to get there well. This was enough for the major, and having also met Gifford's messenger with the note to Captain Maurice, who was not near, and opened it, in which it spoke of his being on the track again, and that he expected to capture the king that night, he felt sore he was also on the track and would try and assist at the capture. He went on carefully up the hill, until near the top he came to a *kraal*, when, in answer to a question for guides, two men started off without speaking or answering any questions, and took their guests to the top of the Ignome Forest, at a place with precipitous edges looking down nearly 1600 feet.

They came to a small open space with long grass, and here the guides put up their hands, and the party was halted. From this point only Major Marter and his interpreter proceeded on hands, knees, and stomach, imitating their guides, until fifty yards further on they could look down and see a small *kraal* of about twenty huts strongly stockaded, standing on a slight rise in the centre, surrounded by forest-covered steep slopes on three sides, and only open towards the south-west. This was the place where the king was then, and a plan was quickly arranged to surround it. The natives were stripped of all their clothes to the skin, and taking only their rifles, *assegais*, and cartridges, were to proceed down the left slope, and get round quietly in front and across the opening, so as to be in time to co-operate with the Dragoons, who were to dismount and lead their horses down, as best they could, any place which was found at all accessible.

The men were all dismounted, and after a little search a place was found where they could get into a little ravine and so work them very carefully to the bottom. The major led, and left the top at 1.45, reaching the bottom at 3 p.m., with the loss of two horses and several men injured. They all say it was most horrible work, all thick forest, with rocky boulders to jump down sometimes several feet. However, *all's well that ends well*, and the end was worth the means; so, luckily, as there was a slight rise hiding them from the *kraal*, which was only 600 yards distant, they managed to mount again *en masse*, and then, directing Captain Gibbing's troops to file off to the right, and Godsden's to the left, they charged at the *kraal* full gallop, and surrounded it before the people inside knew they were there. Fortunately, also, the natives first got across the open, but at the same time others completely hemmed them in.

It was seen that all the men inside were armed; but they were at once warned that if a shot was fired they would he fired into all round, and the *kraal* burnt, so they unwillingly submitted. Major Marter dismounted, and, followed by his interpreter and some Dragoons, went in and demanded where the king was. Umkozana, the last chief who remained with the king, pointed to a hut at the other end, and they went there at once and told Cetywayo to come out. He refused, asked them to come in to him, wanted to know the rank of the officer in charge, and then requested them to shoot him. After some useless parleying, and as it was foolish to lose time, he was threatened that unless he came out they would burn the *kraal*, and not until then did he come out.

The first thing he said was that they would never have caught him if they had not come down the mountains, as he had spies on the flats, and thought it quite impossible for any troops but Zulus to come down the precipices at the back. He was told his life would be spared, but that he must go along with them as a prisoner to the white chief at Ulundi. They captured, besides the king and Umkozana, the headman of the *kraal*, six men-servants and one boy, and five women and one girl; also four Martini-Henry's, lots of cartridges, fourteen other guns, and many relics of the 24th Regiment, with a lot of the king's cooking and sleeping things. The king caused much intentional delay by walking as slowly as he could.

In entering Ulundi six of the Dragoon Guards rode in front, followed by Natal Native Contingent men and one company of the 60th Regiment; then two Dragoon Guards, between whom walked Cetywayo, with another Dragoon close behind him. Natal Native Contingent, eight men of Lonsdale's Horse, and another company of the 60th Regiment followed. Sir Garnet Wolseley did not go out to meet the last of the Zulu kings, as the prisoner had rejected and despised every overture. He was treated, not as a captured king, but as a mere fugitive from law and order.

After a very short delay, the party again started, ostensibly for Pietermaritzburg *via* Rorke's Drift; but the march had not proceeded long, when an express messenger galloped up from the general with an order to proceed with all speed to Port Durnford. When Cetywayo arrived at Kwamagwaza, he said, "This is not the way to the Tugela," and knew at once that he would have to cross the sea. He became melancholy and abstracted. During the entire journey, he retained the quiet dignity for which he is remarkable.

At Port Durnford a surf-boat was ready, into which the king and his party were placed and taken to the steamer *Natal*, which was waiting.[2] The sea was rough, and Cetywayo had to crawl on his hands and knees on board, while one of his people, overcome by the terrors of the ocean, lay on his back in the surf-boat, and made signs that he desired to be killed. The gunboat *Forester* escorted the *Natal* to Simon's Bay, and thence to Table Bay, where Cetywayo and his wives were landed, and were lodged in the castle of Cape Town. Thus ended in a prison in the metropolis of the Cape Colony the career of the last of the Zulu kings and the autonomy of the nation. The greatest and

---

2. The king, the last to get on the gangway, did so by crawling up as the others had done, and when landed on deck gave vent to a sigh, whether of despondency or relief could only be guessed. He would not go near the ship's side, and grasped at the officer's hand to support him while standing on the deck. He was asked to look out to see the anchor weighed, but declined to do so, though manifesting a childlike curiosity about many things on board. Various trappings, such as blankets and mats, were brought on board, the king having two mattresses and two blankets supplied by the military, and the men and women one blanket and mattress each. The prisoners soon became reconciled to their situation on board, and began to manifest much interest in all they saw and heard. A *kraal*, about twelve feet square, was rigged up on the fore part of the poop deck, where there was less motion to the ship and plenty of breeze. The king's women and servants were placed in here with himself, and were made as comfortable as possible. He retired to his *kraal* soon after coming on board, and did not come out till next day, when the officers showed him through the ship. He expressed his great surprise and admiration at many of the things he saw, and was especially struck with the machinery. He would not go down into the engine-room, but gave a token of his wonder at the works of the white men by giving utterance to the peculiar Kafir "Whouw!" He could not comprehend the use of many of the appliances of the cabin, and although be believed the account given to him of how the ship was made, and how much it cost, the processes were a mystery to him and the amount a fable. His first question with regard to the ship was how old she was and "how many cattle she cost." He had a great objection to coming to the Cape, as his spies and messengers had brought up an evil report of the land in times past. Cetywayo exressed his perfect resignation to his fate, and said he knew from the first the war would end as it did, and that he himself would be the sufferer. He blamed his young men, whom he could not restrain at the beginning, and also blamed the English for pursuing the war to its present conclusion.

most powerful ruler of South Africa had defied Great Britain, and in his defeat fell once and for ever all the hopes of domination so long cherished among the native tribes of Southern Africa.

In spite of his large proportions, Cetywayo is a handsome man, of much dignity of aspect. His limbs are large, but symmetrical; very broad chest, large and lustrous eyes, intelligent and not unamiable countenance. With plenty of food and perfect safety, he lost all inclination to be shot. Speaking of the war, he took all the responsibility for the battle of Kambula, but declared that Ulundi was fought against his wish, and in consequence of the determination of his young men once more to try the arbitration of the sword. Now that his power is broken, he laughs to scorn the idea of any more fighting being possible against British rule.

A great meeting was called by the white "*inkosi*" (Sir Garnet) for the 1st of September—the same day, six years ago, on which Cetywayo was crowned. It was fitting that the anniversary of the day of promises never fulfilled should be also a day of atonement. Two hundred Zulus were seated a few paces from Sir Garnet's tent, and although naturally great talkers, the silence of death prevailed. Ranged in rows four deep, with the principal chiefs in front, they listened with perfect attention to the words which decided the fate of their country and of themselves.

Two of the king's brothers and the prime minister of the king were present. At half-past four, Sir Garnet Wolseley left his tent, and, as he walked towards the assembly, was greeted with uplifted hands and shouts of "*Inkose.*" Leaning upon the hilt of his sword, he calmly gazed for a few moments upon the representatives of a conquered nation assembled to hear its doom. Mr. Shepstone interpreted into Zulu sentence by sentence as Sir Garnet Wolseley spoke, as follows:—

It is six years ago on this very day, the 1st of September, that Cetywayo was crowned King of the Zulus, and only yesterday you yourselves have seen him carried away a prisoner, never to return again to Zululand. On the occasion of his coronation Cetywayo made certain promises regarding laws to be observed in the future, which promises he never fulfilled, and his country is now about to be divided into different chieftainships, and I hope his fate will be a warning to all of the chiefs not to follow in his footsteps, but to act according to the commands and terms given by the English Queen, who will most certainly punish any who do not do so.

The interests and welfare of the South African races are very dear to the Queen, and she is anxious that the natives of this country should thrive, as those in Natal have done up to the present time. She will be lenient to faults arising from ignorance; but although inclined, as I have said, to deal leniently when ignorance causes them to commit faults, those who persistently go contrary to good government and peace will assuredly be punished as Cetywayo has been. As they are aware, she lives far away; but her power is very great, and she is quite able to, and will, punish those who take life or make wars contrary to her orders, Cetywayo took the lives of his people for trivial offences, without giving them a chance of defending themselves, or allowing them a fair trial. This must cease.

In future, trivial offences will be punishable by fines. Cetywayo kept on foot a large and powerful army, and did not allow his men to marry without his permission; in future, the young men will be allowed to marry when and whom they like, provided always they have sufficient for the support of a wife, and the consent of the girl's parents. Disobedience of this law is to be punishable by a fine inflicted by the headmen of the *kraal*. As Zululand is almost entirely surrounded by country under the Queen of England's rule, and not threatened in any way, there is no need of a larger army; and in future no guns or ammunition will be allowed to be imported, or to be in the hands of any Zulu.

Nor will any stores be permitted to be landed on the Zulu coast, in case, under the guise of merchandise, arms should be brought into the country. The young men are to be encouraged to labour, and are to be allowed to come and leave when they like; for only by work can they become rich and prosperous. Cetywayo encouraged witchcraft, and what is known as 'smelling out.' That I look to the chiefs to put down, and an end to such ridiculous and foolish practices arrived at. Cetywayo, by this practice of witchcraft, caused many lives to be taken, and neither life nor property was safe. And each chief must clearly understand, before he signs his name to the treaty, that none of his people must be taken without a fair trial before the chief being granted, and the accused being allowed to call his witnesses.

In what I have said there is nothing new, though the young men may have forgotten; but these laws and customs held good before Chaka's ancient laws and usages introduced what is known as the military system. I intend leaving an English officer here as Resident, to be the eyes and ears of England, to watch over the people, to see the laws observed, and that the chiefs rule with justice and equity. I am aware there are still a considerable number of rifles and guns of ours, as well as cattle scattered about the country, and those chiefs who wish to stand well with the English Queen will lose no time in bringing them in and delivering them up to the British Resident.

As they are well aware by their own rules of war and conquest, Zululand now belongs to the Queen of England. She has, however, already enough land in Africa, and so she has, through me as her representative, appointed certain chiefs to rule over districts which I shall presently name. The chiefs elected must remember that this is an act of grace, and that what I am now doing in partitioning the country to various chiefs is only what Cetywayo has himself done in former times. They are well aware our laws, religion, and customs are very different to theirs, and the Queen has no wish to force ours upon them.

As regards the laws and customs they are to be ruled by, they are to be those good and ancient ones in use before Chaka's time; but life and property is to be protected, and no life to be forfeited without a fair trial. As regards religion, there is no wish to force ours upon them, and missionary enterprise will not be encouraged contrary to the wish of the chief and people he proposes to reside amongst. The British Government is very anxious to prevent white people settling in the country, and no sale, transfer, or alienation of land will be permitted or recognized. I consider this a very important point, as in many instances land has been said by white people to have been purchased by them from the Zulus, and given rise to very serious complications.

If, therefore, missionaries do come and wish to reside among the people, all that can be permitted them to hold in land must be a small patch for their house and garden, but none whatever must be alienated from the Zulu people, to whom it really belongs. Some of those I have intended to make chiefs, I am sorry to see, are not here today; but some who are here today will now sign a document, the purport of which I have now told you all; and a duplicate of the treaty will be given to each chief to keep, and a similar one retained by me. The boundaries of the various chieftainships will be told them, and will be clearly defined hereafter by officers sent round for that purpose.

The first division, or coast column, under General Crealock, had not been opposed by the Zulus in the field. It established a series of fortified posts along the south coast of Zululand, opened a new base of supplies at Port Durnford, from which to feed a force operating against Ulundi, destroyed the military *kraal* of Emangwene and the king's old military *kraal* at Ondini, besides clearing the coast district. By the 6th of July, all the great Zulu chiefs, with their' people, from the Tugela River to St. Lucia Bay, had given in their submission. It was the coast column, under Pearson, which gained the battle of Inyezane, and had gallantly held Ekowe for three months; and it was the coast column, more than any other, which had suffered from disease. Among General Crealock's valedictory remarks are the following:—

July 17, 1879.

In notifying to the army in South Africa that Brigadier-General Wood, V.C., C.B., and Lieutenant-Colonel Buller are about to leave Zululand for England, Sir Garnet Wolseley desires to place on record his high appreciation of the services they have rendered, and that their military abilities and untiring energy have materially tended to bring the war to an end. The success which has attended the operations of the flying column is largely due to General Wood's genius for war, to the admirable system which he has established in his command, and to the zeal and energy with which his ably conceived plans have been carried out by Colonel Buller.

BRIGADIER-GENERAL WOOD'S ORDERS.

The Brigadier-General proposes, weather permitting, to leave for Pietermaritzburg tomorrow. In saying goodbye to the soldiers of all ranks, he wishes to express his warm gratitude for the support he has invariably received. The Brigadier-General has gained the commendation of his superiors for the successful operations of the flying column; he feels that the credit he has so obtained has been gained by the courage and untiring devotion to duty of his fellow-soldiers, and he will never forget his comrades of the flying column.

It is right to quote the following orders respecting two distinguished officers of the war:—

> The troops and Naval Brigade forming the first division must be content with the conviction that their gallantry in the earlier part of this war has probably diminished the opposition of the Zulus in this country.
>
> You must be content with the honest conviction that your hard work and energy, under very great difficulties, and with your ranks thinned day by day with sickness and fever, has successfully carried out the task set you by Lord Chelmsford to perform; and, thanks to the valuable assistance and co-operation of Commodore Richards and the Naval Brigade, you have established the landing-place opened at Port Durnford, which will enable further operations towards the capital to be carried out with facility should they become necessary.
>
> Soldiers and sailors of the first division, I thank you all for your good conduct, your hard works; and sympathize with you in the loss of so many comrades whose lives have been sacrificed to this climate, so deadly to man and beast. We have all had great difficulties to overcome.
>
> I wish you all a hearty 'goodbye;' I wish you success and prosperity wherever your duty to her Majesty may lead you. [3]

It would be uninteresting to go into details with respect to the movements of the columns under Colonels Villiers and Baker Russell. Mahabolin and other Magulisin chiefs surrendered, Manyonyoba asked terms of the commanding officer at Luneberg, and the various scattered embers left after the great war conflagration were soon ex-

---

3. The following were the orders as to the movements of the troops:—

To England.

Royal Engineers,—C Troop, 6 officers, 160 men; and 7th Company, 3 officers, 80 men, when transport available. To concentrate at Pinetown when relieved from Transvaal.

Army Service Corps.—750 men, when transport available, concentrate at Pinetown, according as companies can be spared, probably some time yet. All wagons will eventually be sent to England.

Army Hospital Corps.—350 men. To be withdrawn and concentrated at Pinetown, as portions can be spared from duty, into troopships.

Probably England

60th Regiment.—30 officers, 920 men. To sail when transport is available, concentrating at Pinetown

2-4th Regiment.—28 officers, 970 men, 3 officers' wives, 37 women, 57 children. *Ditto, ditto.* (Cont. next page.)

tinguished in the north. In September Zululand was most thoroughly conquered. On the 1st of September, John Dunn, Umgayna, Usibilo, Umcitsobu, Somkelu, and Gonzi signed the terms upon which they accepted chieftainship; Oham and others were proclaimed at a later date. The principal undertakings and conditions were that the chiefs should respect the boundaries assigned; abolish the military system; allow all men to marry and work as they will; prohibit importation of arms; take no life without fair trial; discontinue witchcraft; surrender fugitive criminals from British territory; make no war without the sanction of Government; prevent sale or alienation of land; arbitration to be appealed to in case of disputes with British subjects. The succession to chieftainships to be dependent on approval of our Government.

The following is an exact summary of the terms and conditions signed in duplicate by all the newly appointed chiefs in Zululand at Ulundi, September 1, 1879. The prelude and ending are *verbatim*; terms and conditions summarized:—

I recognize the victory of British arms over the Zulu nation and the full right and title of her Majesty Queen Victoria, Queen of England and Empress of India, to deal as she may think fit with the Zulu chiefs and the people, and with the Zulu country; and I agree and hereby signify my agreement to accept from General Sir Garnet Joseph Wolseley, G.C.M.G. and K.C.B., as the representative of her Majesty Queen Victoria, the chieftainship of a territory of Zululand, to be known hereafter as ——, subject to the following terms, conditions, and limitations:—

To India.

17th Lancers.—24 officers, 455 men, 18 horses To sail first week in October, per *Crocodile* and *Serapis*. Concentrate at Pinetown.

Royal Artillery.—M Battery, 6th Brigade, 5 officers, 157 men; O Battery, 6th Brigade, 5 officers, 157 men. *Ditto.*

88th Regiment.—23 officers, 664 men, 4 officers' wives, 50 women, 87 children. *Ditto.* This does not include two companies at Mauritius.

90th Regiment.—23 officers, 886 men, 3 officers' wives, 35 women, 57 children. *Ditto*

To Mauritius.

91st Regiment.—2 companies, 6 officers, 243 men. Sail first week in October, per *Crocodile* and *Serapis*. Concentrate at Pinetown.

Royal Artillery.—10th Battery, 7th Brigade, 4 officers, 110 men. *Ditto*

To Singapore.

2-3rd Regiment.—26 officers, 800 men. End of September, per *Orontes*. Concentrate at Pinetown.

Terms, conditions, and limitations laid down by General Sir Garnet Joseph Wolseley, G.C.M.G., K.C.B., and assented to by me ———, as the terms, conditions, and limitations subject to which I agree to accept the chieftainship of the aforesaid territory.

1. To observe and respect whatever boundaries shall be assigned to my territory by the British Government through the Resident of the division in which the territory is situated.

2. Not to permit the existence of the Zulu military system or the existence of any military system or organisation whatsoever within my territory; to proclaim and make it a rule that all men shall be allowed to marry when they choose and as they choose, according to the good and ancient customs of his people known and followed in the days preceding the establishment by Chaka of the military system, and to allow and encourage all men living within his territory to go and come freely for peaceful purposes, and to work in Natal or in the Transvaal or elsewhere for themselves or for hire.

3. Not to import or allow to be imported into his territory by any person, for any object whatsoever, firearms, or other goods of any description, and ammunition from any port, inland or sea-coast, and to confiscate all such goods or arms, etc., as come in, fining the owners or possessors of them with heavy fine or such other punishment as may be allowed.

4. Not to allow life to be taken on any pretence without trial before the council of chiefsmen, allowing fair and impartial examination of witnesses in the chiefs presence, and further not to permit of witchcraft or witchdoctors, or "smelling out."

5. To surrender all fugitives demanded by British Government flying from the laws, and to prevent their coming into Zululand, and if in, to exert himself and his people to catch them.

6. Not to make war on any other chiefs without the sanction of the British Government through the Resident of the district.

7. The succession to the chieftainship to be decided by ancient laws and customs, and nominations of successors to be submitted for approval of Government.

8. Not to sell or alienate the land.

9. To permit all people now in the district to remain upon rec-

ognition of his power, and any wishing to leave to be allowed to do so.

10. In all cases of dispute in which British subjects are concerned, to appeal and decide by decision of British Resident, and in other cases not to punish until approved of by Resident.

11. In all cases not included in the above, or in any doubt or uncertainty, to govern and decide in accordance with ancient laws.

These terms, conditions, and limitations I engage, and I hereby solemnly pledge my faith, to abide by and respect in letter or in spirit without qualification or reserve.

Signed at Ulundi on the 1st day of September, 1879.

Chief —— his X mark.

Induna —— *Do*

General commanding Her Majesty's forces in South Africa, and High Commissioner for South-Eastern Africa.

Signed by John Shepstone as witness of the correct interpretation by him and thorough knowledge of the contents of the document the chief has signed.

On the 12th of September Major-General Clifford was able to notify that Colonels Villiers' and Russell's columns were in course of being broken up, after they had thoroughly patrolled the Makulusi district and found all quiet. Oham had returned to his own territory, accompanied by Wheelwright, who was appointed to act as Resident in Zululand. Mongodhla had been driven from his caves and his cattle captured, while his brother had surrendered at Luneburg. Two companies of the 24th Regiment, ordered to encamp at Isandhlwana, removed the last vestiges of the camp, buried any bodies remaining above ground, and erected cairns of stones over the graves of the troops who fell there. More than 5000 guns had been taken, or surrendered by Zulus. Sir Garnet Wolseley did his work thoroughly. Troops were despatched against Sekukini, and Sir Garnet himself proceeded to the Transvaal, in order to subdue discontent among the inhabitants, and establish a settled system of government. It is not necessary to follow him there.

With the conclusion of the Zulu war this book must terminate. As regards the political adjustment of affairs in Zululand, the directions of the Home Government, were no doubt, implicitly obeyed.

The country was made self-supporting in a military point of view, and the chiefs, with their tribes, were so disposed as to form a barrier against hostile aggression. John Dunn, who was a Christian renegade, living as a Zulu in polygamic life, but whose influence was supreme throughout the country, was placed as chief over South-Eastern Zululand. One of his first steps was the prohibition of all missionaries in the country in which he holds sway.

Over Sirayo's country near the border, extending to the foot of the Drakenberg, the chief Hlubi was appointed, about whose tried fidelity and loyalty there can be no question. Oham occupies the region between the Pongolo and the Black Umvolosi. Mnyame, the late king's prime minister, is established near him, and, it is to be hoped, will not hatch plots for the establishment of Oham on the throne of his brother. *Zululand for the Zulus* has been the motto for this arrangement, but hopeless heathenism has been riveted as chains upon the people. Missionary enterprise is discouraged and even forbidden, while all the evils of tribal rule are virtually perpetuated. It has been said with some fancy, but great exactitude, that the new dispensation realizes the description of the country given by Tennyson in *Locksley Hall*—

Never comes the trader, never floats on European flag,
Slides the bird o'er lustrous woodland, swings the trailer from the crag

There methinks would be enjoyment more than in this march of mind.

The passions cramped no longer shall have scope and breathing-space.

Savage women shall be taken to rear dusky races. Polygamy receives approval. Missionaries are forbidden; and, strange to say, all this is really done in consequence of the efforts of the Exeter Hall zealots, who have denounced Sir Bartle Frere and the colonists from the beginning, lauded the heathens, and strenuously objected to any assumption of their territory. The toleration of heathenism is both a blunder and a crime, which, if not stopped in time, must result in disastrous consequences.

Appendix

1.

It is an axiom that history repeats itself, and historical studies, therefore, become particularly useful in a political crisis like the present, when the policy of Sir Bartle Frere towards the native tribes of South Africa has been condemned by the Home Government In all parts of the world a tragedy is enacted when barbarism and civilization come into contact. It was so with the Puritans, whose pioneers landed in North America from the *Mayflower*; it is so with the Dutch and the natives of Java, with the British and the Maoris, with the French and the people of New Caledonia. Wherever, throughout the world, colonization takes place among savages there must be war, or there can be no safety or progress.

When the Dutch formed a settlement on the shores of Table Bay in 1652, it was neither their interest nor their wish to fight, but it was perfectly impossible to avoid it. Although a mere place of call for outward and homeward-bound ships was required, yet it soon became apparent that not merely as a sequence of successful defence, but as a means of protection, it was requisite to annex conquered territory. The *Hottentots* were the first enemies of Europeans in South Africa, and the Kafirs—themselves aggressors—were the second. The latter people were robbers by profession, and an organized system of plunder continually harassed the border farmers of the colony.

The first act of the present tragedy of Kafir war waged against Great Britain took place in 1811, when constant depredations on the part of the Kafirs made it necessary either to repel the enemy or to abandon the country. The latter system of tactics was not then in vogue among the countrymen of Nelson and Wellington, therefore a large force under Colonel Graham was despatched to the front. Land-drost Stockenstrom, who accompanied this force, rode up to a party of the natives and urgently endeavoured to secure peace. In reply he was stabbed to death, and fourteen of the men who accompanied him were likewise murdered.

Of course the Kafirs were chastised, but the snake was only scotched, not killed, and in 1816 the colonial frontier farmers were so plundered by the natives that they were forced to state to Government that they would have to abandon their farms unless effectively protected. As a result, Lord Charles Somerset held a solemn conference with Gaika and other great chiefs in April, 1817, which was followed by a solemn treaty of peace. Those solemn farces must have been sources of im-mense amusement to the savages. Gaika gave pledges with the utmost readiness—there was no difficulty whatever. Honesty and justice were in future to prevail; the people of the *kraal* to which stolen cattle were traced should always be held responsible, and reparation was always to be made *instanter*.

Presents were lavished upon the "Paramount" Chief, and then (in the words of the Rev. Mr. Williams) "Gaika fled instantly to the other side of the Kat River like a thief," plundering was soon vigorously recommenced, and the idea of restitution became almost as great a joke as the treaty of peace. In 1818 the chief T'Slambie positively refused to restore cattle traced to his *kraal*. Afterwards, to gain time, he promised, and then, of course, broke his promise. War was once more forced upon the authorities, and this time the contest was a serious one. While military operations were going on in Kafir*land*, the confederate chiefs got behind our forces, drove in the small military posts, and ravaged the frontier districts. Incited to fanaticism by the witchdoctor Mokanna, or Lynx, 9000 savages impetuously attacked the headquarters of the military at Graham's Town, and it was only by means of desperate fighting that the town was saved.

Soon afterwards another solemn treat; was made, in which it was agreed that all Kafirs should evacuate the country between the Great Fish and Keiskamma Rivers, and that this territory should remain neutral and unoccupied. The usual sequence occurred, the treaty was laughed at and violated by our enemies at the earliest possible mo-ment. Downing Street invariably looked upon the Kafirs in the light of honourable belligerents, and the unfortunate colonists as grasping, unscrupulous men. An outrageous divorce was constituted between truth and justice on the one side, and so-called philanthropy on the other, and the people of the Cape Colony had to suffer the heavy and bitter penalties of this extraordinary ignorance and fatuity.

The course of events from first to last has been very simple. It must be borne in mind that the South African Kafir wars constitute *one* tragedy in various acts, with intervals of unequal duration. The war with Cetywayo is identical in principle with those waged with Gaika, T'Slambie, Dingaan, Kreli, and Sandilli. By immense exertions the tide of savagery has been periodically rolled back, and if wise counsel had been followed, the war of 1835 would have been final; but Downing Street intervened, and it is to the disastrous fatuous policy then adopted that we owe the wars of 1846 and 1852.

It is to this intervention, and to this policy, that we desire in this article, and in others that are to follow, specially to draw attention, because the part taken by Sir Benjamin D'Urban in 1836 is now filled by Sir Bartle Frere in 1879; and the character of Lord Glenelg, who declared that "the Kafirs had ample justification in the late war," seems likely to be attempted by the gentleman who is at present her Majesty's Principal Secretary of State for the Colonies.—April 22, 1879.

2.

The Kafir war of 1835 was exceedingly disastrous to the colonists. Shortly after it had commenced Colonel Smith (afterwards Sir Harry Smith) wrote:

Already are 7000 persons dependent upon the Government for the necessaries of life. The land is filled with the lamentations of the widows and the fatherless. The indelible impressions already made upon myself by the horrors of an irruption of savages upon a scattered population, almost exclusively engaged in the peaceful occupation of husbandry, are such as make me look on those I have witnessed in a service of thirty years as trifles to what I have now witnessed.

The Kafirs were on this occasion, as on every other, the aggressors, and plunder was the principal motive of the war. Fifteen years previously Great Britain had taken the responsibility of settling 6000 of her subjects in the frontier districts of the Cape Colony, and then defence and protection became both the duty and the interest of the home country. With great exertions and after immense loss the war was brought to a close. As a glorious trophy of the war no fewer than 15,000 *Fingoes* were literally saved from cruel captivity. The Moses who led them out of their house of bondage was Sir Benjamin D'Urban, and it was this wise and enlightened Governor who annexed the province of Queen Adelaide, and determined that the liberated people should be placed in this territory, so as to form "the best barrier against the entrance of the Kafirs into the great Fish River jungle." This extensive bush was the "quadrilateral" of the Kafirs, and it was only acquired by the best blood of the British and colonial troops.

During the whole period of the war of 1835 a very small section of colonists had endeavoured to poison the minds of our Downing Street rulers. Their arguments were based on several fictions, including affirmations about violence on the part of colonists having begot violence on the part of Kafirs, and that the great body of Kafirs had never offended us. They even went so far as to make use of glaring untruths respecting Hintza not having been engaged in the war, and misled Lord Glenelg so much respecting the particulars of that chiefs death as to induce his lordship to make use of expressions which he was afterwards compelled to retract.

A steady fire of prejudice, fed by preconceived ideas, constantly existed at home in favour of the Kafir tribes—and indeed all savages—which required very little effort to turn into a consuming fire of anger and indignation. These little efforts were sedulously made *via* constantly continued in South Africa with die most disastrous results. A number of well-meaning and prejudiced men, who can be styled the Exeter Hall party, declaimed with virulence against the colonists, and unfortunately Lord Glenelg was enrolled among their number. This nobleman evidently considered that humanitarian efforts were due to savages only, not to colonists, and through his contemptible folly became the means of inflicting the most severe injuries upon both.

Sir Benjamin D'Urban, who was completely master of the situation, and had proved himself an honest and wise administrator, was entirely ignored, his policy was stigmatized in the most insulting manner, and the sentimental ideas of theorists made to take its place. In a despatch, dated 28th December, 1835, the Secretary of State entirely exculpates the Kafirs and censures both Sir Benjamin D'Urban and the colonists. He says: "In the conduct which was pursued towards the Kafir nation by the colonists, and the public authorities of the colony, through a long series of years, the Kafirs had ample justification of the late war; they had a perfect right to hazard the experiment, however hopeless, of extorting by force that redress which they could not expect otherwise to obtain; and the claim of sovereignty over the new province, bounded by the Keiskamma and the Kei, must be renounced.

It rests upon a conquest resulting from a war in which, as far as I am at present able to judge, the original justice is on the side of the conquered, not of the conquering party." The governor is severely reproved for styling the Kafirs "irreclaimable savages," and the Wesleyan missionaries are also censured. As a sequence the whole country between the Fish and Buffalo Rivers had to be handed over to the Kafirs, although that portion of this territory which extended between the Fish and Keiskamma Rivers had been ceded by Gaika to the colony so far back as the year 1819, and was therefore not conquered in the recent war.

The extraordinary fatuity of this course, judged from a military point of view, is evident from the description of the boundary furnished by Major Charters, military secretary to Sir George Napier. This able officer says: "The line of frontier is all in favour of the Kafirs; a dense jungle—the medium breadth is about five miles—torn and intersected by deep ravines, & great part impenetrable except to Kafirs and wild beasts, occupies about one hundred miles of frontier, following the sinuosities of the Great Fish River. The whole British arm; would be insufficient to guard it." In fact, this country comprised what, by analogy, may be styled the Kafir quadrilateral, or combination of almost impregnable fortresses.

British and colonial blood had to be poured out as water in the wars of 1845 and 1852 to recapture this country; but fanaticism and prejudice are always impervious to argument. "Their blood be upon us and upon our children" is a sentence often repeated in history, so when the Waterloo veteran and gallant British soldier, Sir Benjamin D'Urban, was dismissed for doing his duty, Lord Glenelg defiantly wrote, "You announce to me the abandonment of the province of Adelaide and cast on me the responsibility of all the consequent disasters you predict. I am perfectly ready to take upon myself the sole and exclusive responsibility on this occasion."

It is difficult to find language sufficiently strong to stigmatize the base perfidy and fatuous incompetency of the Glenelg policy. A colony is acquired and its people exchange allegiance for protection; later on 5000 British emigrants are placed in its frontier districts. The savages in and beyond the borders of this country are numerically far superior to our own subjects, and systematically send in plundering bands who devastate the country and impoverish the farmers. It is these savages who make war, and in defence it is at last absolutely necessary either to repel the invaders or to abandon the country.

The case, let it be remembered, is not one of emigrants seizing a country and then applying for protection. It is the British Government which established its sovereignty first and sent its emigrants afterwards. With immense exertion, and at the cost of much blood and treasure, the savage tide is pushed back—and then Lord Glenelg deliberately makes it flow again over the conquered country, perfidiously becomes the ally and friend of the savages and creates a cruel necessity—no other than that of doing the work over again in the bloody wars of 1845 and 1852.

There is scarcely anything in history to form a parallel to this gross injustice and perfidy. Yet at the present moment a large party of fanatical "philanthropists" in England are crying out for a repetition of the same policy in Natal The tide will be pushed back to Cetywayo'a *kraal*, but we must abandon the country after we conquer it. The Zulu King made the war, and it is as purely one of righteous self-defence as any ever waged in the world; yet we are told that the colonists provoked it and are responsible for it! Sir Bartle Frere is to be converted into Sir Benjamin D'Urban! and a new edition of the Glenelg policy must be adopted by her Majesty's Government!—April 25, 1879.

3.

Lord Glenelg emphatically stated that the Kafirs had perfect justification for the war of 1835, and this affirmation was the foundation of his entire policy. He identified himself with the pseudo-philanthropists who looked upon the white inhabitants of the Eastern districts as usurpers and persecutors. The ideas of 1836 remain substantially the ideas of 1879, the only difference being that the *venue* is changed and that the tide of savagery has been pushed further eastward. The settlers of 1820 were placed by the British Government on the frontier of the Cape Colony, and on their part and that of their descendants there was certainly no usurpation, while it positively seems to be the result of monomania to speak of their having persecuted the Kafirs.

The incontestable facts of history prove exactly the opposite: it was the Kafirs that harassed and persecuted them. A comparatively small, struggling, and sparsely settled community was persistently tormented and impoverished by most cruel thefts and constant aggressions, which at last culminated in wars of defence most disastrous to the farmers and the principal portion of the settlers. The stock, dwellings, etc., of the poor border population destroyed in the war of 1835 alone were valued at upwards of £280,000! This was a cruel, terrible infliction on those poor settlers, but it was not considered enough by the Exeter Hall party.

Christianity was blasphemed by a policy of the grossest injustice adopted in its name. Those who were bound by every tie of justice—putting aside charity—to defend their own countrymen turned against them most virulently, and did everything in their power to cause the re-enactment of the bloody scenes in which British settlers in this distant land had suffered so much.

In Mr. Godlonton's "Case for the Colonists" there is abundant proof of the facts already adduced. The Kafirs were the aggressors and the colonists the sufferers. Gross injustice, faithlessness, rapine, and fraud—or in other words, *savagery*—had to be grappled with, repelled, and conquered in the Cape Colony, and the pseudo-philanthropists of England, headed by Lord Glenelg, did everything in their power to aid and assist the latter cause. Perhaps the most clear proof of the error of the British policy on which we are now animadverting may be found in the evidence of one of Lord Glenelg's chosen men and champions. Sir George Napier was sent out specially to reverse the policy of Sir Benjamin D'Urban.

In answer to a Port Elizabeth address, he said,:

I *decidedly* tell you that I accepted the government of this colony in the conviction that the former system, as regarded our Kafir neighbours, was erroneous; and I am come out here, agreeing in, and determined to support, the system of policy pursued by the Lieutenant-Governor of these districts (Captain Stockenstrom) in accordance with the instructions which his Honour and myself have received from her Majesty's Secretary of State (Lord Glenelg).

Nothing can be clearer than this, or more decided; but when Sir George Napier learnt the facts of the case, the mist of prejudice dropped from his eyes. Most fortunately, this officer was an honest man, and dared to give his testimony in favour of the truth in spite of his employers in England. He found that the policy he had been directed to carry out "shocked one's natural sense of justice" (these are his own words), and that he had been completely duped and deceived. Referring to the aggressions of the Kafirs, Sir George Napier says,:

It would not be just to pass over the fact that while much loss has been sustained by the colonists, as stated in the official returns, I am not aware, except in one instance—and that one of no importance—that any aggression has been committed by the border colonists against the persons or property of the neighbouring tribes.

It was at Port Elizabeth, and in the month of October, 1840, that Sir George Napier forcibly admitted that the Glenelg treaties "seem to shock our sense of natural justice, and to be unsupported by any considerations of sound policy." Speaking subsequently to a gathering of the Slambie and Congo tribes of Kafirs at Fort Peddie, His Excellency said:

> You have sustained no bad treatment on the part of the colonists, and I now appeal to you whether the colonists have not kept their part of the treaties ever since they were made? I ask if there has been a single act of injustice of which you have any reason to complain on the part of the Government and the colonists? You will answer. None. I therefore appeal to you for justice towards the colonists.

In fact. Sir George Napier was forced to thoroughly change his opinions, and it is unnecessary to multiply proofs of this well-known fact. Would to God that Sir Michael Hicks-Beach, or even Sir Charles Dilke, could come out to South Africa and report to the Home Government so as to avert the awful catastrophe of surrendering conquered Zululand to Cetywayo! This would be a suicide greater in extent and more terrible even in its consequences than the surrender of the province of Queen Adelaide by Lord Glenelg. But surely if the world had been searched no more reliable man than Sir Bartle Frere could have been chosen. He is a most upright, wise, and experienced administrator; the friend of her Majesty the Queen, and himself distinguished for all the qualities which make men respected and trusted. He belongs to the "Aborigines' Protection Society," and is in all respects above suspicion, yet his moat positive assurances weigh lightly in the balance against the monomania existing among certain classes in Europe, that savages must be right and colonists invariably wrong. It is a bitter reflection that Zulu savagery finds its best allies among the very people from whom we spring, and that the most deadly enemies of the white people of South Africa are literally "those of their own household."

One of the most able newspapers in South Africa echoes the sentiments of Lord Glenelg, Dr. Philip, and Bishop Colenso. It declares against annexation, and also against interference with the usages of the native chiefs. It is said that to rule the Zulus through their chiefs is the policy of her Majesty's Ministers. The extraordinary admission is added that "order will be found better than caprice and the law better than individual notions of right." Surely we must admit that the rule of chiefs is purely a rule of absolute caprice, and that the history of Cetywayo's government specially proves it. The will of the monarch is the law of the land, and bloody sacrifices constantly connected with witchcraft are purely the effects of cruel and avaricious caprice.

The entire history of South Africa shows the folly and cruelty of the policy advocated by the enemies of Sir Bartle Frere. No careful student of Cape history can fail to see that the Glenelg plan of non-annexation was most disastrous, while it was only when the power of the Gaika and Gcaleka chiefs had been finally taken from them—and not till then—that the people of this country, whites as well as blacks, could hope to be finally released from the fearful curse of recurring thefts, bloodshed, and wars. In fact history teaches plainly that to secure peace, prosperity, and happiness to all the people of Southern Africa it is absolutely necessary:

(1.) To secure territorial guarantees, such as those justly acquired in a war of defence by Sir Benjamin D'Urban.

(2.) To create a firmly knit and strong confederation of colonies and states in which the Queen and just laws shall be supreme, to the exclusion of witchcraft and the caprice of chiefs.

Incidentally, we may be permitted to illustrate what is really meant by this "rule of chiefs." Everyone knows that diabolical and wholesale slaughter is a characteristic of the rule of all Zulu potentates. Dingaan, Panda, Cetywayo, are all alike in this particular. It is the system as much as the men that we have to blame. Perhaps there is no more distinguishing proof of constant cold-blooded and revolting cruelty arising directly and constantly from the rule of chiefs than in the administration of the laws of witchcraft One example out of hundreds is sufficient. Missionaries from time to time publish most revolting cases, but they are all of the same type, and merely as a sample we refer our readers to the one alluded to by Mr. Godlonton, at page 99 of his *Case for the Colonists*.

The son of a chief was sick, and a. man of property was immediately selected for torture and death, simply because the witchdoctor said that it was under his evil influence that the sick man was suffering. He begged and prayed for instant death, but of course that boon is never granted. First of all the victim was held to the ground, and several men pierced his body all over with Kafir needles, two or three inches deep. The victim bore this with extraordinarily resolution, and his tormentors became tired, complaining of the pain it gave their hands, and of the needles or skewers bending. By this time a fire was kindled, into which large square stones were placed to heat.

His wife having first been cruelly beaten and ill-treated, the victim was brought to the fire, laid on his back, with his feet and hands tied to pegs driven into the ground. When the stones became as hot as possible, they were placed upon his groin, stomach, and chest. Then the scorching and broiling of the body went on, the stones occasionally slipping off, and being immediately replaced and held on by sticks. These awful tortures lasted from 10 a.m. to 6 p.m., when the unfortunate victim of the benefit of the rule of the chiefs in South Africa breathed his last, We are asked to perpetuate this system, and to surrender any conquered country in Zululand, so that savagery may still continue without interruption, and we may reap in Zululand from the policy of 1879 the fruits obtained in 1845 and 1852 from the Glenelg policy of 1836.—April 29, 1879.

4.

The great question of Sir Bartle Frere's native and Zulu policy is easily narrowed. His Excellency believes in abolishing the power of chiefs, and in obtaining after defensive war adequate territorial guarantees. The opposite policy has, undoubtedly, caused the wars of 1845, 1852, and 1877. The relinquishment of the province of Queen Adelaide by Lord Glenelg necessitated its reconquest, and the system of endeavouring to rule through the medium of chiefs has resulted in disastrous failure. A chief is necessarily antagonistic to civilization: all his power, influence, and means are obtained from savagery, and it is this latter system it is his interest to foster and to continue. But for the astuteness and ability of Sir George Grey Kreli would undoubtedly have thrown us into a serious war in 1857.

This great chief ordered cattle to be slaughtered in such a manner as to prove that he had even determined to "burn his ships." Emissaries were despatched to Moshesh, to Taku, and to the Tambookies. A witchdoctor was used as a tool in the usual manner, so as to stir up the people by means of superstition, and the system, whose continuance is advocated by a party, only failed because of the checkmate movements of the Governor. Subsequently, it was purely the continuance of the system of the chiefs that led us into the war of 1877. If their power had been abolished, as it should have been, great calamities would have been averted from their own people and from the Cape Colony.

A careful honest study of colonial history is all that is necessary to prove to demonstration that weak half-measures with Kafirs are as irrational and absurd as they are cruel. When we conquer we are bound to take away entirely the pernicious powers of the chiefs, as well as to retain such land guarantees as are really necessary for future safety. Those who advocate this sound, wise policy are real philanthropists, substituting justice and sound ideas for theoretical ideas, founded for the most part upon that worst description of ignorance which is founded upon prejudice and preconceived ideas.

One argument brought forward against Confederation is based upon the lowest possible motives. It is the pockets, not the heads or hearts, to which this earnest appeal is made. One great Government in South Africa with provincial administrations will really be too expensive! Besides, an objection is taken to the removal of the liability under which the British Government labours at present. Let the Home country continue to lose its beat blood and treasure rather than we should lose our money. A great strong Confederation would put an end to Kafir wars by putting an end to the possibility of their success, but lest we should have to pay a few more taxes the British ratepayers' purses and the British soldiers' bodies must continue to bleed.

This infamous policy is not worthy of the Colony of the Cape of Good Hope. We have attained our majority as children of the Empire, and we must be prepared to resume our own responsibilities. These, unquestionably, include self-defence, and to make that efficient the fable of the bundle of sticks most be exemplified in the close union of all our states and colonies. Nothing is more clear than the fact that all South Africa is like a draught-board—the blacks are on one side, the whites on the other. There is no separating the interests of either combatants, so that when Cetywayo fights against Natal, he fights against this colony as well as against the Transvaal and the Orange Free State.

But real economy is always attended by a sound and statesmanlike system of Government. There would be no recurrence of native wars under Confederation, and this alone would be a source of great economy and great prosperity. South Africa, not Downing Street, would conduct its own native policy, and there would be then no fear of the recurrence of such a policy as that of Lord Glenelg. At present we are not safe, and the sooner such a period of incertitude and danger is terminated the better for the taxpayers here and in England. Are the people of this country not able to govern themselves in a Confederation? The history of the separate states and colonies proves the contrary. If we are able we ought to be willing, as such a union means against the natives invincible strength, and consequently both peace and economy.

Above all things we ought to relieve ourselves from the curse of being perpetually exposed to the meddling and muddling of our native policy. Fatuous incompetency, such as that of Lord Glenelg, is quite enough to ruin half a dozen colonies, and we really can never be quite sure that it will not be renewed.

A reference to Sir Bartle Frere's instructions proves very clearly that his Excellency had incomparably more power than any previous Governor-General or High Commissioner, and in acting as he did under *carte blanche* authority, in no way exceeded his powers. He had to choose between allowing the Zulu despot to make war when he wished and in what manner he chose, or in checkmating him by early action. The latter policy has been adopted with Cetywayo as it was with Kreli, and in spite of a temporary check will be the means of effectively protecting the interests both of the British colonists and the British crown. England never had a more faithful or conscientious officer than Sir Bartle Frere, and a time will come when on the page of history his name, with those of Sir Benjamin D'Urban and Sir George Grey, will be blazoned as the greatest and most enlightened statesmen who ever ruled in Southern Africa.

After me, the Deluge, would have been a convenient and very safe motto for each of these men, but they scorned the wretched time-serving policy of shunting off the evil day from themselves so as to allow its calamities to accumulate into terrible magnitude and burst with awful force upon their successors. But the principal defence of Sir Bartle Frere's action and policy is to be found in his despatches, and to them we earnestly beg careful and impartial attention.

The people of the Cape Colony and Natal are composed of many races and of many creeds, but with the most insignificant exceptions they all declare in the most emphatic manner in favour of the policy of Sir Bartle Frere.

> *Saxon and Celt and Dane are we,*
> *But all of us Danes in our welcome of thee.*

From Capetown to the Tugela River and from L'Agulhas to the Orange River one universal shout of sympathy and approval goes forth to England. Resolutions, earnestly and emphatically declaring that the High Commissioner is right, are sent to the foot of the Queen's throne from Capetown, Port Elizabeth, Grahamstown, Graaff-Reinet, Pietermaritzburg, D'Urban, and hosts of smaller places. The newspaper press, with very few exceptions, constantly and vigorously declares aloud the public sentiments. Surely all this is a powerful argument. The people of South Africa, whose lives, property, and character are at stake, may be trusted to take such a lively interest in the entire subject as to understand it thoroughly. Their interests and those of the United Kingdom are thoroughly identical in this matter, and the sky does not so change the mind even in this portion of the British Empire as to pervert entirely the moral nature of so many of Her Majesty's loyal subjects.

Political events connected with the Zulu war form incomparably the moat powerful argument that has yet been adduced in favour of South African Confederation. We really cannot afford any further Glenelg experiments, and so soon as we can knit ourselves together in a powerful dominion we are by no means apprehensive of the expense of fighting our own battles. In the first place we would take care that there would be no chiefs to fight with, and that witchcraft, tyranny, and other abominations should finally cease. The natives would have to learn the habits of industry and peace, and would be induced to substitute spades and ploughs for guns and ammunition.

A just, firm policy of this character, would form a basis for Christianity, peace, and civilization, whereas the senseless and fatuous plans of so-called philanthropists are as destructive to the natives as they are injurious to the colonists and to the British Empire of which they form a part.

It would be fortunate for South Africa if fair play were as much the practice as it is the boast of Englishmen, There are many men at home full of the same sentiments of righteous indignation as those which animated Sir George Napier previous to his arrival in South Africa. How few are there like that Governor, who will consider it their duty to make themselves conversant with the subject, and then be guided by their conscientious convictions.

The cause at issue is simply savagery *versus* civilization, and before a verdict is given the entire evidence and arguments ought to be attentively heard and carefully considered. Colonists do not desire war, but an end of all war. They are most anxious to save, not to destroy, the savages, and the wise statesmanship of such men as Sir Benjamin D'Urban, Sir George Grey, and Sir Bartle Frere is absolutely necessary for this purpose.—May 2, 1879,

IMPORTANT DESPATCH FROM SIR BARTLE FRERE.

The following despatch from Sir Bartle Frere, dated Pietermaritz-burg, February 12, has been issued as a parliamentary paper:—

Sir,—In my despatch of January 24th last, I only partially an-swered your despatch of December 18th. I was, in fact inter-rupted while writing by the intelligence of our disaster at the headquarter camp on the 22nd, and was obliged to close my unfinished despatch to be in time for the mail. The very seri-ous check which we received on the 22nd does not, however, seem to me to call for any modification in the opinions I had already ventured to lay before Her Majesty's Government; on the contrary, it seems to confirm most strongly the arguments I had already advanced in my despatch of the 24th, to show that it was impossible, with any regard to the safety of these colo-nies, to defer placing in the hands of the general commanding her Majesty's forces the enforcement of the demands made on Cetywayo.

Deeply as, in common with every subject of Her Majesty, I de-plore the disastrous check we have received, it is impossible to shut one's eyes to the fact that it was, in all human probability, mainly due to disregard of the general's orders that so great a disaster occurred; whilst every circumstance accompanying or following the events of that day proves what an insecure posi-tion we occupied both here and in the Transvaal with such a neighbour along so many hundred miles of undefended fron-tier.

As a consequence of the crippling of Colonel Glyn's and Colo-nel Durnford's columns, and the shock which has been given to the colonial forces, Europeans as well as natives, the columns of Colonel Pearson and Colonel Wood have been obliged to sus-pend their advance and await reinforcements, which can only be looked for to the extent required from more distant parts of South Africa and from England. It has become painfully evi-dent that the Zulu king has an army at his command, which could almost any day unexpectedly invade Natal, and, owing to the great extent of frontier and utter helplessness of the undis-ciplined hordes of Natal natives to offer effectual resistance, the Zulus might march at will through the country, devastating and murdering, without a chance of being checked, so long as they abstained from attacking the entrenched posts of Her Majesty's troops, which are from fifty to a hundred miles apart.

The capital and all the principal towns are at this moment in 'laager,' prepared for attack, which, even if successfully resisted, would leave two-thirds of them in ashes, and the country around thoroughly desisted. From every part of South Africa outside the colony, where the native races predominate, come the same reports of uneasiness and of intended rising of the native race against the white man; whilst the majority of the Transvaal European population is in a state of avowed readiness to take any opportunity of shaking off the yoke of the English Government.

It may be said that these are only the stronger reasons why hostilities should not have been commenced with the Zulu king. But I submit that every circumstance which has lately occurred shows how impossible it is to defer hostilities for more than a few weeks at the utmost, possibly till the harvest now ripening was gathered, and till the Tugela was fordable. The feeling which has just burst out, both among native tribes and in the Transvaal, was there already, and in the Transvaal, at all events, its expression could not have been deferred by any postponement of hostilities with the Zulus. But what possible chance was there that Cetywayo himself would for any length of time have remained quiescent within his own borders? He had not acknowledged officially, and in the usual form, the award of the disputed territory in his favour, nor had he condescended even to discuss the terms of the High Commissioner's messages to him.

Had Lord Chelmsford's large force been kept permanently on his frontier, he might possibly have refrained from action as long as this force remained. But its permanent retention was not, as Cetywayo knew, probable, and the removal of the force would assuredly have led to a renewal of the encroachments and the violations of the territory which he had directed or acquiesced in during the preceding year and a half; the slightest accident might have led to a collision taking us at a disadvantage, and what he had the power to do in a colony so little prepared for self-defence may be judged from what he has done since Her Majesty's troops crossed the border.

It seems to me vain, I had almost said criminal, to shut our eyes to the fact that there has grown up, by our sufferance, alongside this colony, a very powerful military organisation, directed by an irresponsible, bloodthirsty, and treacherous despot, and that as long as this organisation exists and is so directed it is impossible for peaceful subjects of Her Majesty to feel security of life or property within fifty miles of his border.

The existence of this military organization makes that of a peaceful English community in his neighbourhood impossible, and unless Cetywayo's power of murder and plunder be restrained, this colony can only continue to exist as an armed camp. Again, it may be said that before attempting to coerce Cetywayo the presence of a large force in the field should have been secured. To this I can only answer that though a larger force might undoubtedly have lessened the chance of successful opposition, there was no reason whatever at the time to suppose that the force at our disposal was too small for the task attempted. I will not dwell on what might have been the case had orders been obeyed, and had things happened otherwise than they did happen.

I stand on the broad fact that I sought information in every possible quarter, and had, and have, no reason whatever to suppose that there was anything rash in the undertaking. I know of no one who is supposed to know the Zulus whose advice had not been as fully heard as I could obtain it. Of the three persons who, among unofficial as well as official authorities, are supposed beat to know the Zulus, their feelings and probable intentions, one expressed to me his own belief in the ultimate acceptance of the terms offered without fighting; another considered we had, in our military calculations, greatly overestimated the Zulu power; and a third, who had perhaps better means of judging than anyone else, whilst agreeing that the Zulu power had been much overrated, was convinced that the Zulu people themselves would bring their tyrant to reason, and that, after a single action or two, the military system of the Zulus would collapse.

It is a singular coincidence that the latter opinion was expressed to me on the 22nd, at the very time that our camp at Isandala was in possession of the Zulus. Looking back on the past in the light of what has happened, I cannot think the work was rashly undertaken. But even if I could have hoped that farther reinforcements could be expected within a reasonable time in answer to a call for them, there was no time to wait No one who had carefully studied the events of the last two years, and knew the ways of these barbarians, could reasonably have expected the Zulus to remain quiet, and it was clear that, even if they deferred action, there were elements of strife elsewhere which could not be evaded or delayed.

As I have said before, and in other communications, the die for peace or for war had been cast more than two years ago. It was a simple question whether we should steadily bring our differences to an issue on a clear and unmistakable demand for our right to live at peace with our neighbours, or whether we should await the convenience of the Zulu king, and be taken at disadvantage when he saw his opportunity. It seems to me that this same principle of self-preservation and self-defence should be steadfastly adhered to in all our future proceedings.

It may be quite possible to patch up a peace with this or that tribe, which shall for the time be more or less satisfactory to some of the interests in this or in a neighbouring colony. But I submit that Her Majesty's Government should not permit peace to be made till her Majesty's unquestioned supremacy has been established and recognized by all Zulu tribes who now acknowledge Cetywayo between this and the Portuguese territory around Delagoa Bay. This I firmly believe to be the only guarantee for peace, security, good government, and progressive civilization throughout Her Majesty's possessions and all neighbouring territories In South Africa; and without such security I feel assured that this colony of Natal can never be a safe residence for peace-loving and civilized men of European descent.

H. B. E. Frere,
Governor and High Commissioner.

LEONAUR

ALSO FROM LEONAUR
AVAILABLE IN SOFTCOVER OR HARDCOVER WITH DUST JACKET

AT THEM WITH THE BAYONET *by Donald F. Featherstone*—The first Anglo-Sikh War 1845-1846.

STEPHEN CRANE'S BATTLES *by Stephen Crane*—Nine Decisive Battles Recounted by the Author of 'The Red Badge of Courage'.

THE GURKHA WAR *by H. T. Prinsep*—The Anglo-Nepalese Conflict in North East India 1814-1816.

FIRE & BLOOD *by G. R. Gleig*—The burning of Washington & the battle of New Orleans, 1814, through the eyes of a young British soldier.

SOUND ADVANCE! *by Joseph Anderson*—Experiences of an officer of HM 50th regiment in Australia, Burma & the Gwalior war.

THE CAMPAIGN OF THE INDUS *by Thomas Holdsworth*—Experiences of a British Officer of the 2nd (Queen's Royal) Regiment in the Campaign to Place Shah Shuja on the Throne of Afghanistan 1838 - 1840.

WITH THE MADRAS EUROPEAN REGIMENT IN BURMA *by John Butler*—The Experiences of an Officer of the Honourable East India Company's Army During the First Anglo-Burmese War 1824 - 1826.

IN ZULULAND WITH THE BRITISH ARMY *by Charles L. Norris-Newman*—The Anglo-Zulu war of 1879 through the first-hand experiences of a special correspondent.

BESIEGED IN LUCKNOW *by Martin Richard Gubbins*—The first Anglo-Sikh War 1845-1846.

A TIGER ON HORSEBACK *by L. March Phillips*—The Experiences of a Trooper & Officer of Rimington's Guides - The Tigers - during the Anglo-Boer war 1899 - 1902.

SEPOYS, SIEGE & STORM *by Charles John Griffiths*—The Experiences of a young officer of H.M.'s 61st Regiment at Ferozepore, Delhi ridge and at the fall of Delhi during the Indian mutiny 1857.

CAMPAIGNING IN ZULULAND *by W. E. Montague*—Experiences on campaign during the Zulu war of 1879 with the 94th Regiment.

THE STORY OF THE GUIDES *by G.J. Younghusband*—The Exploits of the Soldiers of the famous Indian Army Regiment from the northwest frontier 1847 - 1900.

www.ingramcontent.com/pod-product-compliance
Lightning Source LLC
Chambersburg PA
CBHW021103090426
42738CB00006B/480